THE ULTIMATE MOUNTAINS

Frontispiece (overleaf)

Where Tibet, Nepal, and India meet on the Roof of the World. The view in
monsoon cloud from 19,000 feet on Panch Chuli

The
Ultimate Mountains

AN ACCOUNT OF FOUR MONTHS'
MOUNTAIN EXPLORING IN THE
CENTRAL HIMALAYA

by THOMAS WEIR

with four maps and 48 pages of photographs
by Thomas Weir and Douglas Scott

CASSELL & CO. LTD

LONDON

CASSELL & CO. LTD

37/38 St. Andrew's Hill, Queen Victoria Street
London, E.C.4

and at

210 Queen Street, Melbourne
26/30 Clarence Street, Sydney
P.O. Box 9, Lower Hutt, N.Z.
Kingswood House, 1068 Broadview Avenue, Toronto 6
122 East 55th Street, New York 22
Avenida 9 de Julho 1138, São Paulo
Galeria Güemes, Escritorio 518/520 Florida 165, Buenos Aires
Haroon Chambers, South Napier Road, Karachi
15 Graham Road, Ballard Estate, Bombay 1
17 Central Avenue P.O. Dharamtala, Calcutta
P.O. Box 275, Cape Town
P.O. Box 1386, Salisbury, S. Rhodesia
P.O. Box 959, Accra, Gold Coast
Calcada Do Carma 55-2o, Lisbon
Klosterstrasse 34/36a, Düsseldorf
25 rue Henri Barbusse, Paris 5e
Islands Brygge 5, Copenhagen

First published 1953

15496

Set in 12 pt. Walbaum type and
printed in Great Britain by Butler & Tanner Ltd., Frome and London
F.552

CONTENTS

ILLUSTRATIONS

Where Tibet, Nepal, and India meet on the Roof of the World.
  The view from Panch Chuli   *Frontispiece*

Dunagiri schoolchildren do their work at 11,800 feet. The school-master seated cross-legged was very much the " master " here
Dunagiri Bhotias
These little girls have unusual caste marks
Loading the jopa, a job requiring strong teeth
This rather handsome " jopa-wallah " prepares his chapatties
Approaching Malari village on the Dauli with our jopa train
This little girl of Malari is beyond the scope of the expedition's " Health Service "
Lampak base camp. Scott shows off some of Goria's exquisite chapatties while McKinnon and Sangia look on
The north face of Tirsuli, 23,210 feet above the Uja Tirche glacier

Between pages 62 and 63
The pinnacle ridge on Uja Tirche, 20,350 feet. Climbers near the base of the central pinnacle
Uja Tirche
The camp on Uja Tirche. Kamet, 25,447 feet, stands high above the Badrinath peaks
Pinnacles of Uja Tirche
Camp on Uja Tirche, looking into Tibet
Camp on Uja Tirche, where the dividing line between India and Tibet is cut by the sheer sides of the Girthi Gorges
South Lampak peak from the camp on Uja Tirche
View from Camp 3 at 17,800 feet on South Lampak.
Madbir and Nurbir had to forage far to keep the base camp at Lampak in fuel
Taking advantage of an off day to make pancakes
Bhotias and pack-laden goats crossing over the shoulder of Uja Tirche to contour into the Girthi Gorges

Between pages 78 and 79
On the crest of the pass. Fixing the girths of the saddle-bags before dropping into the Girthi
The Girthi, a world of naked rock rising sheer, 7000 feet from the river
Sometimes hands as well as feet were needed as can be seen from the sort of country shown here
The third ravine in the Girthi Gorges
The bridge across the river to the Girthi settlement
In the Himalaya the rush of water is such that the stream bed moves with restless force, making footing difficult. Scott is being assisted over by a Bhotia

With fur bonnet on his head, the wild shepherd stands back while
    the sahibs and coolies inspect a sheep offered for sale
Camp on the Tibet border near the Unta Dhura Pass
Loading the sheep
The saddle-bags have been smeared with dung to keep the sheep
    from nibbling
Tibetan and Bhotia
Clad in sheep-skins and long boots this wild-looking figure draws his
    sword with a smile
Leonard Moules, missionary, in his little dispensary at Milam
A corner of Milam village

Between pages 86 and 87
Tom McKinnon who left us at Milam to try the crossing of Trail's
    Pass
The coolies used their rest days in Milam to good purpose by making
    themselves new trousers and adding length to an outsize bedmat
Sangia is proud of this pullover he has finished. Another is already
    on the needles
Perimal spinning on the march
The dancing girls of Milam sway to the rhythm of weird music
On the Ralam Pass
A telephoto shot of the Yankchar Pass showing the peaks Chhiring
    We and Suli Top behind
On the crest of the Ralam Pass at 18,470 feet showing the downward
    route
The Panch Chuli range from the base camp
Camp 2 on Panch Chuli
Near Camp 2 on Panch Chuli we came across this settlement, a
    couple of primitive huts on the edge of the glacier
Camp 4 on Panch Chuli. Monsoon clouds welling up over the
    Tibetan peaks
The glacier at 19,000 feet and the ice walls of Panch Chuli

Between pages 92 and 93
The skirts of Panch Chuli
Camp at 19,000 feet on Panch Chuli
The north col, Panch Chuli
Murray and Scott are fêted by the Bhotias of Yansu
This is the favourite instrument of the Bhotias. Unfortunately this
    one had only two working notes which gave it a certain monotony
The last of Panch Chuli

SKETCH MAPS

CHAPTER I

Beginnings

IT was Scott's idea that we go to the Himalaya. To every mountaineer it is the ultimate, but during the war Scott had penetrated the high foothills to see at close range snow peaks of the mightiest mountain chain in the world.

Often since his return to Scotland in 1946 he had spoken to me about it. Wistfully he told me of the joys of Himalayan travel ; of paths which climbed ridge after ridge of foothills, to contour profound gorges, and wind a way through enchanted woods where all sorts of wild birds sported ; of camps at 12,000 feet on flowery alps, surrounded by glaciers and peaks of Himachal—peaks unclimbed, many unexplored.

Now, at last he wanted to do more than talk. He was out with a plan. His eager finger traced a line on the map, and I caught the magic of strange names, legendary names, that had the ring of adventure in their very sounds —the Rishi Gorge, Nanda Devi, Dunagiri, Bagini, the Girthi.

We need have no unwieldy organization. With a third man and the minimum of food and equipment we could travel light, live off the country, and really go places. Had not Dr. Longstaff described this territory of Garhwal and Almora as not only the most beautiful of the whole Himalaya but abounding in opportunity for the mountain traveller, from unexplored gorges to great clusters of

1

unclimbed peaks, 20,000 feet high and more ?   Now was
the time to go if we were prepared to live in the present
and abandon the long-term security of good jobs.

That was in the autumn of 1949.   Came February 1950
and nothing had been done beyond sounding the ideal
third man, Tom McKinnon.   He was keen, but his business
as a pharmacist prevented him from making positive plans.
On the understanding that he would come if he could get
a locum, I booked three berths on a ship due to sail in two
months' time.   The ship was called the s.s. *Himalaya,* a
good omen in itself.

It was then we invited W. H. Murray to lead the
expedition.   Murray is an author by profession and had
just finished the hard task of writing a book.   We knew
he was set to go to Greenland in the summer, but thought
India's icy mountains might have something for him that
Greenland's had not.   My first intimation that he was
coming was a wad of closely-typed foolscap detailing jobs
for all members of the expedition, an unusually high
proportion of them seeming to fall on Tom Weir.

Scott had to work out detailed mountain plans and on the
basis of these I had to plan food and transport.   McKinnon
was asked to produce the medical supplies, while Murray
obtained the latest intelligence and co-ordinated our efforts.
Thanks to Murray's flair for administration things went
smoothly if hurriedly, and by early April we were ready
to begin packing.   To our joy, McKinnon had found a
locum and was coming with us, so we were a Scottish
Mountaineering Club party of four.

There was only one worry at the back of our minds, and
that was political.   We needed a mysterious document
called an " Inner Line " pass, to enter the area of the
Tibet-Nepal border where it forms a great angle with
India in the districts of Garhwal and Almora.   Explorers
had been held up, and even turned back, by not being in
possession of this pass.   Despite help from the highest
British sources, and repeated air-mail letters, we could

not wring as much as a reply from the Indian Government. With or without the pass, our minds were made up to go. The man who said that it is more pleasant to travel than to arrive had certainly not crossed in the dust and glare of midsummer the twelve hundred miles that lie between Bombay and the foothills of the Central Himalaya. Not that the time taken on our trip was excessive. The journey took only forty hours from the sea to Kathgodam railhead, and that included an engine breakdown plus a five-hour halt in a blast-furnace temperature of a hundred and twenty degrees, a heat I never want to feel again.

It was a great moment when the green foothills reared above the haze—real green—like a memory of Loch Lomond's woods in a desert. For that is the best comparison I know to fit the parched Indian plains in this wilting period before the monsoon.

Soon we were off the train, where a lorry should have been waiting for us. Instead, it was another trial of patience ; but finally we were off, climbing steeply through dense vegetation on a good macadam surface.

Zig-zagging upwards, we emerged from the jungle to find ourselves high above terraced fields. None of the ground being flat, the natives have cut steps into the hillsides, the steps getting smaller with the steepness of the slope, so that a field may consist of no more than a strip twenty feet by four. Most of the fields were parched brown, but in the places where water could be carried, potatoes and vegetables showed a rich green.

Climbing higher we came amongst lilac trees and exotic flowering shrubs. From green banks by the roadsides wild flowers sprouted in profusion. Looking back after fifty miles or so, one saw sharp little peaks, moraine-like, terraced from top to bottom in a two-thousand-feet sweep. The houses were built into the slopes like boulders.

After the plains, it was delightful to feel the hot wind grow gradually cooler. Flickerings of lightning and the low rumble of thunder showed the mountains were making their own weather, and soon a dust storm was blowing. As we pulled into Essex House, Ranikhet, storm clouds were discharging the first rain we had seen since leaving Glasgow. As transport officer, this should have been, for me, a night of celebration. We were at our base, and our half-ton of expedition stores was safely deposited indoors, nothing missing. But my celebrations took the form of four shots of M. & B. tablets and a salt and water gargle. A thermometer stuck in my mouth registered a hundred degrees, and the local doctor's diagnosis was that I was suffering from a combination of heat stroke and tonsillitis. But I had enough faith in the Weir constitution not to be downhearted.

To awaken after a much-needed sleep is good at any time. To suddenly become aware of wave after wave of green mountains stretching across the horizon is the cure for any sickness. I was soon out on the lawn in my pyjamas. Beyond the bordering flowers of the garden the crests of these high jungle foothills caught the slanting sunshine, and incredibly above them, like silver writing in the sky were the snows—Nanda Ghunti, Trisul, Maktoli, Nanda Devi, Nanda Kot, and a peak we recognized as our first objective, Bethartoli Himal, above the Rishi Gorge. Such a mighty range of mountains baffled the imagination.

Our immediate need was coolies to transport our stores, but bouts of shivering and sweating prevented me taking any hand in their selection. We wanted eighteen. Murray opened negotiations, and after much bargaining a contract was arranged and a parade of the men held.

They were a ragged-looking band, far from prepossessing in appearance, with torn and patched homespuns, and girdled with the carrying-ropes of their trade. Mrs. Fergusson, who had been our adviser in so many things, stood by to assist with the language, for as yet none of us could speak Hindustani. These men were Dhotial tribesmen from Nepal.

We were not ordinary tourists, they were told. We would be travelling hard and climbing high. We would be away for several months and would require some, but not all of them, for the whole time. Most of them would be sent home after three weeks. Were they willing to come on that basis?

Their eagerness to join us was heartening. To a man they volunteered, and I was glad the job of rejecting four supernumeraries out of the total parade was Murray's, not mine. The unfortunates who had to be discarded were downcast, and refused to leave the parade till ruthlessly hauled out by the headman, Kuar Singh.

An advance of pay all round, and we said our " salaams ", on the understanding that our coolies would join us in the morning for the forty-mile run to Garur and the true beginning of the expedition.

CHAPTER II

Into Garhwal

GETTING under way on an expedition is a hectic job. Loads have to be rearranged in convenient weights for carrying. Final kit for march and mountain has to be sorted out, and everything has to undergo a last-minute check to ensure that nothing vital is left behind. At 11 p.m. we hammered the last nails into our crates and retired. The loads were ready for transport. My prayer was that my temperature, which had been going up and down like a yo-yo, would be sufficiently far down to enable me to start.

It was. With joy we loaded our stores aboard the bus, glad to be off at last. It was a fascinating, not to say exciting, run to Garur. The way lay at first along the crest of a ridge. Below us was a wide valley of terraced fields, and rising over it were ridges, rising in successive waves to the silver of the whole Garhwal chain, all of them clear and seen to scale against this sea of valley and jungle.

Winding through trees and flowers the scene changed most excitingly every few minutes. Gradually, round fearsome twists and bends, with much tooting of horns, we lost height crossing the Kosi river where wheat was being harvested, making a more colourful landscape of fields with their gold of grain crops and green of potatoes, and blossoming trees and shrubs. In the hottest part of the day we pulled into Garur to dump our gear beneath a great tree.

Coolies and sahibs of the expedition. *Back row L. to R.* : Goria, Perimal, Sangia. *Centre row* : Weir, Scott, Murray, McKinnon. *Front row* : Pakir, Madbir, Nurbir

Essex House, Ranikhet, the starting point of the journey. The author chatting to Mrs. Ferguson who gave the expedition so much valuable help

Into the foothills. The hundred-mile journey to the Rishi Gorge begins

On the crest of a ridge above Lohajang. The bell is rung by passing travellers to scare away lingering "devils". Nanda Ghunti, 20,700 feet, rises ahead

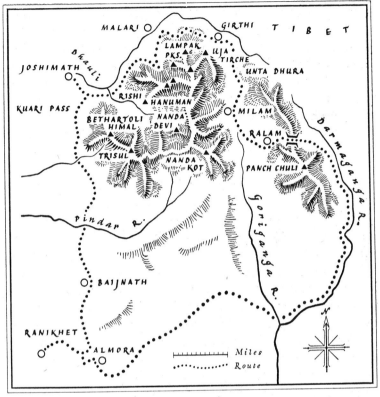

THE EXPEDITION'S ROUTE

We were down to 3000 feet now and the heat felt tropical. We would begin the march when it cooled.

Meantime we had to suffer the attentions of the village males, senior and juvenile. They flocked to stare at us in a way that made us eager to escape their scrutiny. If we had any self-consciousness then, it was to be dispelled before long. The white man in the Himalaya is what the monkey is to the zoo. One must learn to quell any feeling of annoyance but preserve a quiet dignity. In preparation for the move we sorted out the gear into eighteen loads of sixty pounds each.

It was then we saw the mettle of our headman. He was a rather wizened, spindly-legged Dhotial, much given

B

to cringing in the presence of his superiors. We had not a very high opinion of Kuar Singh. Now we saw him come to life. He rounded up his men, called each one by name, and undid our handiwork by pulling the loads to bits and rearranging them. We protested, but he disregarded us. The wisdom of his technique was shown when each man had gone and there was nothing left for him to carry. We thought it a crafty move and made mental note that we would straighten out this piece of injustice.

The walk was attractive, only three miles long, and I had someone to carry my pack for me. This business of Himalayan travel certainly had something. Over the river, past Baijnath temples, and then ahead of us was a shapely little peaklet called Dungoli. We climbed to it by a path of wild flowers and cactus, through woods and along a ridge to find a dak bungalow. The situation was superb, with an outlook across the whole valley to the high tops, now partly in cloud. We had cause throughout our travels to bless the men of imagination who sited these bungalows in such heart-filling situations.

We had been told by some Himalayan travellers that Dhotials were unreliable coolies who would never stay with us, were useless on high mountains, and would certainly not cook any food for us. Kuar Singh gave the lie to the last charge forthwith. He delved in kitbags, produced our whistling kettle, and in no time served us with lemon tea, chapatties, soup, more tea, and biscuits. Moving about with a kind of stealthy creep he contrived a self-effacing look even when his back was turned.

Sitting happily on the veranda we looked out on a wall of black cloud from which came low rumbles of thunder. In the stillness before the deluge a golden oriole sang its repeated liquid phrase. Grey tits, green-backed tits, and drongos, played around us. Then came the storm with a fine lightning display and magnificent roars of thunder.

Morning was delightful. Low mists and a damp fresh-

ness in the air like a morning in Scotland. Kuar Singh
had pressed cups of tea into our hands before daylight so
that we were on the move by 6 a.m. We had not only a
most excellent headman but a veritable Jeeves and Mrs.
Beeton rolled into one.

The way led down to a glen and along its floor for a
while, then a gradual climb through woods and terraced
fields. Gradually the sun was dispersing the high clouds
to reveal fragments of snow peaks and jungle ridges. The
wonderfully cool air lasted until about 8 a.m. when the
sun broke through in full strength to light up wheat fields
busy with workers and chase every cloud out of the sky.

Our route lay along a narrow ridge which rose through
woods to the Forest Rest House of Gwaldam at 6000 feet.
The time was only midday, and despite the flies, it seemed
the height of luxury to lie and rest, or enjoy the sight of
the strange birds which flitted round the bungalow—bush
chat shrike, scarlet minivet, jungle crows, white vultures,
hoopoe, and hedge robin. The position of this Rest House
makes it one of the finest view-points in the Himalaya,
but the snow peaks were cloudy and a flat light lay on the
nearer ridges.

I was ready for Kuar Singh's cup of tea in the morning.
My throat felt as dry as cardboard and jagged as broken
bottles. As dividend there was a sore stomach. But the
sight of Nanda Ghunti and Trisul silhouetted against the
pale sky chased away all mournful thoughts. Gradually,
snow became visible on the peaks which brightened to pink
as the first sunlight touched them, then turned immediately to silver. There is nothing lingering about a Himalayan sunrise. In quick time the warmth was on us and
the vast landscape of jungle ridges reared against the
glittering peaks in green waves.

To start a march downhill is to start the day well, and
the changing views of descent to the Pindar river and a
new valley gave expectancy to every bend of the path.
Terraced hillsides dropped to the valley, to be lost as one

cast one's eyes upward to the tangled jungle and hanging glaciers of the near snow peaks. From the ridges of Nanda Ghunti, Trisul, and Maktoli, a long snow plume told of wind high up. Round by a long up-and-down curve, across the Pindar, and we wound by Dewar and its temple, to shelter for a couple of hours from the fierce heat of the day. " *Pina pani* " (drinking water) was the cry here. It was the first Hindustani I had learned to croak, and if I had a nickname among the coolies it might have been these two words. They watched my salt-water gargles with well-bred interest, but my frequent swigs at the bottle never failed to raise a grin.

Afternoon, and we started up the pass to Bagargad. This was a most beautiful stretch, with cloud shadows rolling over jungle hills and yellow corn making a fine splash of colour in a thousand feet of terracing. At one little village the population turned out to stare at us, the women with their jewellery hanging on their noses and ears, and anywhere else it could be hung or fastened, the men grinning hugely in the most friendly way. Our house that night was no more than a little bothy on the edge of a hill burn. The chill in the air testified to our gain in height.

The morning miracle was getting away by 6.30 a.m. But Kuar Singh daily sorted order out of chaos, and this morning we started with a climb to a pass, a narrow pass on the crest of a ridge where hung a bell and a little shrine with votive flags. The coolies prayed and rang the bell, then sat down to admire the view. I cannot believe they were unmoved. Straight in front of us, incredibly close, Nanda Ghunti seemed to drop straight into jungle, its ice walls gleaming in a sweep of thousands of feet.

Travelling down for a long way by a steep path, we contoured the Wan glen, passing odd travellers with their water buffaloes, sheep, and goats. They stared at us without restraint. Some would follow on behind us, stopping when we stopped. Invariably we were asked for cigarettes, but being non-smokers we had to refuse. (What cigarettes we had were packed away, to be issued to the coolies when their supplies gave out.) They were obviously unsophisticated types unlike the Kumaonis we had met earlier on the march. These people wore homespuns, the main item of which was a folded blanket, fastened like a Scottish plaid with a silver pin. This garment, worn over knee-length trousers, was the receptacle for various personal belongings, from kukris to hubble-bubble pipes, and combined the functions of jacket, rucksack, and sleeping outfit. The men had a kindly, open look, which we liked, but their women seemed dispirited drudges who hardly looked upwards from their toil as we passed.

In rain we reached Wan, an amazing green place distinguished by tall cyprus trees. The place seemed alive with birds, cinnamon thrushes, Himalayan tree pie, plumbeous redstart, red-headed tits, rufus turtle doves, and a host of other things. As usual the bungalow was pitched high above the village.

That night we opened our first dispensary. Our first patient was an old man, almost blind, who expected his sight to be restored. Then the coolies showed their scars. By which time the old chap was back, this time with his goat. McKinnon, our pharmacist, examined its throat, produced iodine and applied it to a wound there. But the old man was not satisfied. He craved something more for himself, so we gave him a few stomach pills. Fascinated by our medical skill, he had to be driven away, or he would have attached himself to us for the remainder of the expedition.

The spidery-legged Kuar Singh had been far from happy these few days past. His self-effacing creep had to be done on sore feet for his shoes were killing him. He wore brown shoes, rather smart brown shoes, much too narrow for Dhotial feet. Several times I had urged him to throw them away, or walk bare-footed like the others. But his dignity as headman would not allow this. Now he presented his feet for inspection and they were a sorry sight. The prince of bunions was developing on his right small toe, and both heels were bloody. I picked up his shoes to throw them away but the look of horror which came over his face stayed my hand. He crept around that night bare-foot as other men.

Whether we liked it or not we were going to have another day in Wan. The coolies needed flour for their chapatties and no Himalayan village carries a surplus sufficient to feed eighteen coolies for long. The rough grain would have to be ground to flour and that would take all of a day. McKinnon and Scott were greatly pleased, for above us was a peak called Jatropani. New snow had fallen on it since our arrival, and its height of 13,000 feet promised exciting views in all directions. They decided to climb it.

Despite sore throat and temperature I tagged along at six o'clock the next morning. It was beautifully cool and the bird song of this glen reminded us of home. We climbed to the crest of the pass, then through jungle to emerge on a real alp, an oasis of green where little primulas were blooming, starring the ground with yellow, pink, and blue.

Following the ridge we cleared the trees at about 11,000 feet, enjoying on the way fascinating views of Nanda Ghunti and Trisul, Nilkanta and the Badrinath peaks. Framed by remnant clusters of mauve and red rhododendron blossom, we could only speculate on the sight of this place in early spring when the whole hillside to Wan is abloom.

Stimulated, we pressed on. The peak itself was like a Scottish mountain, with long snow-filled gullies coming down from a rocky corrie. McKinnon raced ahead, apparently not feeling the altitude. But Scott and I had already " had " our wonderful moments on a truly abominable climb. We moved with the steps of men suffering from a hangover.

Such a weariness has never been mine on a mountain

before, and a summit never so far away. Lolling on top, I felt my peak of mountain ambition reached, even if my tongue was too swollen with thirst to voice it. In Scott's face I saw reflected my own feelings. And this at a lower altitude than we were used to in the Alps. Meantime McKinnon was on his second top and off to the third by the time we came away.

Water was my craving on the descent, any kind of water. I found it in a bamboo thicket and plunged my face into it, forgetful of dysentery or any other warnings. A mug of tea on getting into camp was nectar indeed after ten hours on the peak. The coolies had put in their time profitably by buying and killing a goat, and I arrived in time to be fêted by Kuar Singh in a culinary triumph of potatoes, rice, liver, and goat-flesh.

But, so far, I have not mentioned the animosity which existed between Scott and Kuar Singh. Scott is not at his best in the morning. He likes to come to life gradually, not with a cup of tea in his hand. He was embittered against breakfasts which started with tea and finished with porridge of every consistency except the right one. But he was never up early enough to stop Kuar Singh and promote the correct dispensation of these things. And his Hindustani, like ours, was unequal to explaining such a difficult subject. So Kuar Singh, instead of being greeted with smiles of welcome, got nothing but a string of curses from the " chota sahib ".

The march next day began with such a cursing, and Kuar Singh crept away baffled. It was a hard march, over the Wan pass, then a steep descent to the Nandakini river, past the village of Kanol. Jatropani had given my tonsillitis its quietus, and I moved with enjoyable vigour.

Under a veranda the village school was in progress as we passed. The pupils sat cross-legged on little mats with their slates on their knees, but as soon as their teacher spotted us, he called them to their feet. With heads bent and hands clasped as though in prayer they stood respectfully till we passed. Their teacher was little more than a boy of fifteen years of age. He had no English so was unable to respond to my attempt at having a chat.

In this wilder country we were now entering, the people had a natural dignity and poise which impressed us. The houses were better built and the general lay-out was neater. The track followed a ravine of astonishing steepness, winding amongst bluffs to drop in steep scree to a flat place by the Nandakini river.

Hemmed in by rock bluffs and jungle we unrolled our tent for the first camp. We had heard that Dhotials will stand around and let you wrestle with a tent and make no attempt to assist. As soon as our tent appeared they sprang into action. Ours was a complicated tent, but in quick time they had the hang of it. The tent up, they retired to a cave in the rocks while we were besieged by hordes of tiny biting flies. Settling on food in a black mass, attacking our ankles and elbows, they drove us to the river for a bathe.

Towards dusk our camp was invaded by another throng, a great string of natives who promptly squatted on their hunkers to stare at us. They were a wild-looking crew in their blanket homespuns, puffing at great pipes, and twisting raw wool from their wrists on to spinning bobbins. One man with hardly any English elected himself spokesman, but it was a one-sided conversation in which the request for cigarettes was prominent. We were glad when they moved off.

The next day's march to Ramni was notable for the backward view of the way we had come. The succession of passes we had followed was clearly visible. Below us the ground dropped away so steeply that a stone could actually be hurled across the gorge to land on the other side. Our camp at 8000 feet was on a delightful shelf below steep crags.

Scott and I enjoyed this camp. Dashing over the crags, a brown falcon, about the size of a peregrine, gave a

spirited flying display, and soaring overhead were the
largest birds of the Himalaya—lammergeier and griffon
vultures. Eagles look small by comparison with these
enormous birds of eight and nine feet wing-span. Around
our camp the Himalayan whistling thrush sang in thin
wild notes. Among the other wild life was a scorpion
which Kuar Singh had rooted out from the shed where
he proposed to sleep.

The climb to the Chechni Binak at 10,510 feet was
delightful. A low mist hung on the hillsides, creeping
among the bamboo and tall rhododendrons and refresh-
ing us by its cool moisture. The birds rejoiced, and we
saw many things, Himalayan tree creepers, woodpeckers,
minivets, and the orange-splashed, blue and white of a
monal pheasant as it crashed with squealing sounds through
the undergrowth.

It was even finer over the other side, dropping through
an enchanted wood matted with rose-like flowers in white
bloom. A green alp called the Sem Kharak invited camping, but we overruled the wishes of Kuar Singh and pushed
on. It was a place for lingering.

It was soon obvious why they wanted to camp. The
going became very hard. Far below us was the river,
roaring between overhanging rock bluffs. The coolies cut
straight downhill to it. Scott and I took a more circum-
spect line by a track marked on the map, but we reckoned
without a landslide which had wiped it out in a vital place.
Mistakenly we climbed upward instead of downward,
following another path till stopped by an impossible bluff,
below which, a thousand feet down, we could see a bridge.

This cost us much trouble, and in rain and thunder we
eventually gained the bridge, determined in future to pay
more heed to the coolies. The uphill slog that followed
was about equal to the half-way mark on Ben Nevis. But
half a chapattie and a barley sugar sweet gave us enough
zip to enjoy the climb. From up here we had a view of
the Gohna Tal lake with its enormous scar showing the

landslide that had caused it. Looking down the way we had come, and up again to the pass of the morning, one could only feel astonishment that such a country should have paths at all. Kuar Singh did not exaggerate when he said we had done two marches in one.

The Kuari Pass at 12,140 feet was the lodestone of this hundred-mile march. Frank Smythe had described it as one of the great view-points of the world, and our spirits were high as we topped the first 10,400-foot pass. Immediately ahead, rose a wall of peaks that might have been the North ridge of Glen Coe. There was no mistaking the col, a tiny gap between rocks and snow gullies, hanging woods filling the corrie leading to it.

Down 1000 feet to a deep-cut gorge by a landslide, past a huge waterfall, and we began the climb in a series of zig-zags. Grazing under the trees of a grassy alp in this lonely place were flocks of sheep and goats. Squatting on carpets by piled saddle-bags, their herds played cards while the cooking pots simmered on the fire. It seemed an ideal life, and I hoped they appreciated their good fortune in a world of such peace and beauty. A few hundred feet more and we were at our camping place.

This was a pleasant hollow. The coolies were disposed out of sight in a variety of caves, but we could hear their laughter and the cheery crackle of their fires. 2000 feet above us was the col. Southwards a wealth of forest and crag, a natural game reserve. We had seen no animals, but such a country must be alive with panthers, wild bears, and woodland deer.

To be up on the pass at sunrise promised great things, and Scott and I promised ourselves a four o'clock rise. But it was nearly seven before we got off, heavy rain and clouds making us later than usual. There was no view from the top. On this north side the pass was well covered with hardish snow, a slip would have resulted in a long slide in many places. The coolies were sure-footed and crossed confidently.

It was Scott we were worried about. He was walking like a drunken man, unsteadily and very slowly. A sore throat and sickness were his complaints, and below the snow line he collapsed. McKinnon took him in hand with doses of chlorodine. It was a hard descent, but the chlorodine did the trick and kept him going on the 6000 feet down to Tapoban in the Dauli valley.

We were in an entirely different kind of country now. Ahead of us, rock peaks rose sharper and higher than the Chamonix Aiguilles, rising out of gorges wilder and more impressive than anything in the Alps. With a thrill we saw the great cleft of the Rishi Gorge with the pointed crag of the Lata peak showing the thousands of feet we would have to climb to penetrate its depths.

Towards it we contoured, dropping through Tapoban to reach a little Rest House above the river. It was locked, but while we waited for the key, we put Scott in his sleeping bag and took his temperature. McKinnon told him it was a hundred, but it was a hundred and four. He quickly fell asleep with hordes of black flies buzzing round his head.

CHAPTER III

The Rishi Gorge

IT appeared we were to be denied the hospitality of
the Rest House despite our sick man. The Chowkidar
demanded a permit before he would open up. We had
no permit, but we hung on hopefully. Our saviour was
a half-mad Yogi wearing the cloth of a holy man.

He denounced the Chowkidar. Pointing a skinny arm
at him, and raising his wispy-bearded figure to his full
height, he proclaimed us the " Guests of India ". What
else he said we will never know, but the door was slung
open and we were invited to enter. The Holy Man stayed
for tea.

The exaggeration of his manner and his peculiar laugh
had given a clue to madness. It was confirmed when he
told us he had been released from Calcutta Asylum. He
spoke some English and used it to tell us about his religion.
His ideas were sound : love, universal love, one brother-
hood in spirit being the real things. He spoilt his good
work by shameless scrounging of cigarettes, food, and
shoes.

Next day was hectic. Scott was up and about, his temperature restored to normal after M. & B. tablets and a
long sleep. We had to sort out food and stores necessary
for three weeks' climbing in the Rishi Gorge. The scene
of wild disorder in the small bungalow was unbelievable.
Crates had to be emptied and repacked, and their contents
listed. Nothing that could be left behind was to be taken.

And while all this was going on there was worry at the back of our minds. The coolies had delivered an ultimatum that we should keep them all for the whole trip or they were going home. There was some misunderstanding somewhere, but how to put it right not knowing the language ?

It was then Providence took a hand. The Chowkidar appeared in great excitement to turn us out. Important sahibs were arriving and we were occupying their quarters. The sahibs were a party of government officials headed by Mr. Hartwell P. Singh, agricultural officer. Having introduced ourselves as the Scottish Garhwal Expedition we were invited to remain as the " Guests of India ".

But the part that Providence took was in sending a man like Singh to act as interpreter for us. The coolies were summoned and we had a parley. Tactfully Singh showed them how impossible it was for us to keep eighteen coolies on a long climbing trip, when for long periods we could employ only half that number. The conversations went smoothly and at the end of it perfect agreement was reached. The real trouble was that none of the men wanted to leave us. We needed only six permanent coolies. They all wanted to be among the six. So much for the story that Dhotials would never stay with us.

Singh knew the Dhotials better. Although desperately poor and compelled to earn their living like pack horses, their honesty was beyond question. They were away from Nepal for four or five months usually, during which time the local shopkeeper or headman supplied food to their dependent wives or families, on the understanding that it would be paid for on the return of the coolie. While deploring the lack of opportunity which prevented them bettering themselves, he was glad that such men were available in the Himalaya. We could only echo that sentiment.

Dr. E. L. Chowfin, Professor of History at Allahabad University, who was also in the party, told us something of the pilgrim traffic which goes up and down the Alaknanda Valley a few miles away. Sixty thousand pilgrims are estimated to pass through the Hindu shrines of Joshimath and Badrinath each season. These were described by the Professor as sub-humans with no ideas about anything except saving their souls.

To die on pilgrimage is to achieve the ultimate glory, hence no hardship is too great for them. Hindus worship as many gods as there are saints in the Roman Catholic religion, with the further advantage of being able to have as many as four wives. Some hill people have more, but Dr. Chowfin put them down as nature worshippers rather than Hindus.

By Tapoban's hot springs we said farewell to our Yogi friend. I produced the camera to take a photograph, at which he stripped naked and went through the postures of Yoga, the position of meditation, controlling hunger, breathing, etc. Religious men of his type have sat in barrels in Britain.

Our way lay up the Dauli, a glen at first, rapidly becoming a gorge. Wherever one looked dark rock peaks jutted against blue sky. Across the Rishi torrent by one swing bridge and back across the Dauli by another, and we found ourselves in an impressive spot. On the north side slabs rose for thousands of feet to rocky tops. Deep down, the cataract formed a rainbow, while a great water-fall cascading over rocks for hundreds of feet glistened like silver.

Mingling with the roar of the torrent one caught the songs of whistling thrushes. Blue rock pigeons nested on ledges above the river, and in a little niche between stones I found the nest of a plumbeous redstart. Down at the riverside we saw our first white-capped redstarts, and grey wagtails flickered on long tails.

Our destination was the village of Lata, eight hundred feet above the path, on the slopes of the Lata peak. Up there we were welcomed by the whole village and escorted

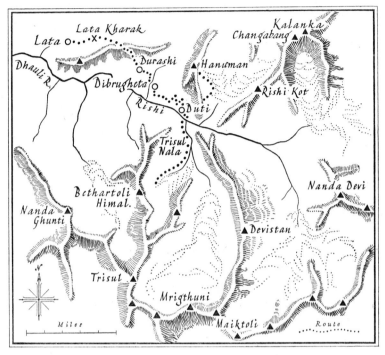

THE RISHI

to a camp spot on a ploughed field. The situation was good, but the grit and flies which found a way into everything made the place far from comfortable.

We were glad to escape next morning and leave Murray to the task of buying in a supply of flour and lentils. Our task was to find a way on to the Lata Kharak, 4000 feet up the jungly crags of the Lata peak. The box canyon of the lower Rishi Gorge has not yet been breached, and though we were urged to solve the problem, we preferred to enter the upper gorge by the route found by Longstaff, and subsequently followed by Tilman and Shipton when they penetrated the Inner Sanctuary of Nanda Devi.

The route began with a long upward traverse to an amazing alp perched on top of a pinnacle, on which sheep were grazing. We spoke to the shepherd but he shook his head when we pointed to the slope above. In the absence of local knowledge we pressed on. Almost at once we struck a rib which led us upwards for 3000 feet to clear the trees on the ridge.

Opposite us was Bethartoli Himal, 20,840 feet, so close that we could see its enormous cornices and hanging ice-falls. It was the most impressive peak in the landscape. Nanda Ghunti and the Ronti peak seemed insignificant beside it. The north ridge on which was pinned our hopes looked difficult, crevasses and a steep ice step combining in the final sweep. Also, we saw it was a more complicated peak than we had imagined. Its solution was certainly going to be an interesting problem. Meantime the question was how to get to the bottom of it. The rock peaks above the Rishi rose like a comb.

Across the Dauli the view was no less impressive. Its great rock walls were dwarfed by ice-plastered aiguilles, Matterhorn-shapes, and a variety of fierce snow peaks. Up here little Alpine plants were blooming on the edge of snowdrifts. We made a brew of tea and revelled in our situation. The true col we would cross lay 2000 feet above us, and although rocky and seamed with gullies it did not look difficult. McKinnon, a most expert route finder, was careful to cairn the way down. Back in camp, Murray was packing away the grain and flour, having had a busy day.

Thanks to our reconnaissance, we put our tent on the crest of the ridge within four hours of leaving in the morning. Again, Bethartoli Himal was clear, so Murray was able to look and give us the benefit of his judgement. Leaving us, he started up towards the col. Visibility was failing and the atmosphere was thundery.

At dark there was still no sign of him, but we refused to worry. The coolies had not the same faith in his mountaineering skill. They hung round the tent with anxious faces, then started up to look for him. He came

Himalayan path between the Nandakini Gorge and Ramni.   Note the tiny figures of the coolies

The half-mad Yogi of Tapoban

The road to Lata up the Dauli Valley from Tapoban

in about 7.30 p.m., absolutely all-in, reporting that the going was pretty bad. He had been deceived, like us, by the innocent-looking slope above. There was much more rock and snow than one supposed. Also, there appeared to be four passes, so that each one had to be investigated. Only when he proved the first three false, did he discover the correct one. On the descent he had contoured lower down, to become entangled in prickly shrubs. His weakness was due mainly to hunger, for except for a few sweets he had eaten nothing since morning. Cold had been his main enemy, for he wore only a bush shirt and flannel trousers.

Following a keen night, we were away early to traverse across rhododendron and steep snow gullies so hard-frozen that steps had to be cut to allow a passage. It was telling work, up and down over tangled vegetation, with a final pull over rock and turf, then up a snow gully. It took us five hours for 2000 feet, in contrast to four hours for 4000 feet the day before. The peak of Dunagiri looked very close from here, like a greater edition of the Dent Blanche.

But we had little time to admire views. Ahead of us the wall of the Rishi dropped for thousands of feet in rock and snow, a narrow ledge showing us the start of the route. The take-off was good, but soon we had to provide a rope handrail to safeguard the coolies, and try climbing higher to find a better terrace. This proved so exacting that one of the coolies dropped his load. It disappeared into space never to be seen again. We were too relieved that it was the baggage, and not the porter, to worry. But although we did not know it then, that loss cost us our chance of climbing Bethartoli Himal. A weeks' supply of food had gone at one stroke. None of us had seen verticality on such an enormous scale, the gloom of clouds emphasizing the Rishi depths at the foot of these impassable, box-canyon walls.

The strain was telling on the other men. One was

c

violently sick and the rest were complaining of head pains. Unfortunately there was still a lot of up and down work across the face before we reached a stony gully which led by a long descent on grass, then up to a broad alp where a trickle of water emerged from some snow. To crown this satisfying moment, the sun came out from behind clouds and shone warmly on us as fires were lit and a " hoosh " prepared. The coolies certainly had our admiration, and in honour we issued tea and cigarettes. A noggin of brandy inside us prepared the way for a good sleep. The lower Rishi was behind us. Tomorrow we would look into the upper gorge.

Our situation might have been high up in a Scottish corrie. In the morning the ground was white with frost, and above us the Dharashi pass rose to a grassy saddle. In a flood of sunlight we climbed to the col, to meet the most inspiring prospect any of us had ever seen. Standing above the rock walls of the Rishi was Nanda Devi. The other peaks of the basin were insignificant beside this Queen of Mountains. Draped in the pale green of ice, skirts shadowed, the Blessed Goddess held her shining head in a halo of cloud. Incredible that such a mountain could be climbed. Looking at the tremendous sweep of the south ridge, we doffed our balaclavas to Tilman and his party for their great performance in climbing it.

Below us was the Rishi itself, and our task was to get down a subsidiary gorge leading into it, cross it, then contour its walls. Scott and McKinnon made off to climb a 16,000-foot peak for a view. Murray and I started down with the coolies. Fifteen hundred feet of steep descent and we were pulled up by gorge walls. Murray went forward to reconnoitre. I waited for his shout to call us on. An hour passed and there was still no shout. On the assumption that no news was good news I motioned the coolies forward.

Descent went well, to a point forty feet above the torrent, where rock slabs fell sheer to the water. Telling the coolies to wait, I started down. It was horrible stuff to climb on, shaly rock overlaid with earth in places, which peeled off when pressure was put on it. A slip meant a long drop over an overhang into the gorge. Before I could stop them, the coolies had started down. From below it looked extraordinarily precarious. I wanted to go back up with a rope but they refused its aid. It was a relief when they were all down.

Above us the slope was not quite so unprepossessing. It was more jungly, and the rocks were cleaner cut, not quite so slabby. This time I climbed up and fixed a rope. A few hundred feet through forest and we emerged on Dibrugheta alp to find Murray having a siesta.

Dr. Longstaff had described Dibrugheta alp as the most beautiful place in the Himalaya. We could imagine nothing more superb. Ringed by pine woods we were in a grassy hollow alive with flowers and birds. Everywhere we looked there were rock peaks. It was the camping place of camping places. But there was no water.

Reluctantly we plunged down to a second gorge to camp amongst jungle. The embers of an old fire showed this camp site had been used by other expeditions. As usual some of the men stowed themselves away in caves, others preferred to pitch our high-altitude tents.

It was a happy night in camp. McKinnon and Scott had climbed their mountain. We were well into the Rishi Gorge, and at this jungle camp we could have enormous camp fires. All of us were pretty fit except Murray, who had not been quite himself since his heroic reconnaissance of the Lata Kharak. He looked worn, but with his constitution we knew he would soon pick up.

Morning saw us climbing a thousand feet through timber to get on to the clearer ground above. We were in view of Nanda Devi again, and over a welter of crag and forest below us was the Rishi torrent. The ground we were on was thorny and rocky, but nothing to the wild tangle of shrubs and cotoneaster that lay ahead. This drew blood from the coolies' feet and tore unmercifully at their ragged pants, so that it was a wonder they had any pants at all at the end of the day.

Traversing up and down, dropping hundreds of feet, and climbing over a thousand feet at one point, we landed at last on a desert of broken rocks dropping to the Rishi. The problem was to get down and to find a camp spot. McKinnon and Murray went ahead on a downhill traverse, avoiding crags where possible. We camped that night in the thick of the woods two hundred feet above the river, a haven of rest after an exhausting day.

It had been an interesting march from the bird-watching point of view. We had seen a grey-headed fantail warbler, an attractive little thing with sulphur yellow underparts and eyestripe, dark mantle, and an engaging habit of spreading its tail like a fan. There were flocks of snow pigeons, twisting white with the sun on their wings, and an attractive little sprite, the blue-fronted red start, a bird blue on the back as well as on the front, but with an orange breast and fiery rump. All we had seen of the four-legged animal kingdom were a few musk deer.

Now we came to the sad task of dismissing the surplus coolies. The money bags were opened, and the whole assembly formed round the tent. They were all good lads, but three had proved outstandingly good, Perimal, Goria, and Sangia. Without hesitation we selected these three. And if Sangia had a quiet smile, then he was entitled to it for we had nearly turfed him out at Ranikhet as being too old.

Selecting the other three was not so easy. In the end it boiled down to three distinctly jungly wallahs with the names Madbir, Pakir, and Nurbir. These three had kept themselves very much to themselves and were fine carriers. As a rock climber Madbir was a tiger.

The other coolies could scarcely conceal their disappointment at not being chosen, especially a little fellow who had appointed himself orderly, and greeted us at times with a beautiful salute. But he was not in the class of the jungly wallahs as a climber and carrier.

Kuar Singh got a shock when he heard we were dismissing him. We were sorry to part, but this country was too hard for a man of his age. Despite sore feet and the most killing of marches, he had placed our interests first at all times. We complimented him on being an excellent headman and a first-rate chap. His profound " salaam " showed he appreciated the compliment. Long after it was dark the men hung round the tent, anxious to prolong this happy occasion.

By the time the porridge was boiled in the morning, the coolies were ready to take off for the return journey to Lata. We shook hands with each man in turn, and thanked them for their good work. The next job was to weigh our food in order to estimate our climbing time in the Trisul Nalla. It was a blow to discover we were a hundred pounds down on ata and rice. As this loss exceeded our calculations by fifty pounds, I decided as from now, I would supervise the cooking and minimize this source of leakage.

As it was, we dumped eighty pounds of food in a cave and loaded the six coolies with the remainder. " Loaded " is the word, for the weight was excessive for the country we had to traverse, steep jungle, thorns, loose scree, stones, all of it up-and-down work.

A final crash through five hundred feet of jungle and we were on the boulders of the riverside opposite the Trisul Nalla. The job before us was to get across the fast-flowing Rishi. A good bridge would have to be built, for anyone unlucky enough to fall into the river would be dead meat in quick time. After reconnaissance to find the best place, we got to work cutting trees, or, to be more correct, we started it and the coolies took over. Our three hand axes, bought in Argyle Street, Glasgow, for a few shillings, had soon knocked down a couple of birches and a pine tree.

The target for the first log was a large boulder projecting into midstream. McKinnon directed operations. A rope was tied to the pine tree and it was stood on its end, the idea being that we should lower it on to the boulder by the rope. All went well till the full weight of the tree came on the rope, when its momentum caused it to bounce off the boulder and be swept away in the Rishi, to be hauled ashore for another try.

After trying this a few times the coolies showed us how. Using a light tree they swung it across. With this as a guide the heavier log was slid over it, ropes from a high position on the bank holding it in position. Scott then crossed with a rope round his waist and soon we had the three logs lashed together and weighted down with boulders.

A flash of lightning and a roll of thunder accompanied the last load across. No sooner was the tent down on the gravel than heavy rain ushered in the threatening storm. The coolies seemed very pleased with themselves and sat round the fire, a groundsheet suspended from a boulder above them catching the heavy rain.

It was still raining when we rose in the morning, to pack up and begin the last traverse into the Trisul Nalla. We took a bad route, steep and difficult, calling for the use of the rope in many places. After being forced in the wrong direction for a time we managed to turn the rib and found ourselves confronted by ravines. We had kept high above the river to this point, but now the jungle forced us down. Miraculously the going became easy, and following the glacier stream we emerged at the foot of Bethartoli Himal.

Although the time was only 2 p.m. we were pretty weary. There was a camp site, and the sun came out to warm us for the first time that day. Murray pushed on, hoping for a higher camp site, but when the coolies arrived it was obvious we would not get them further. With their heavy loads they were quite spent. Further, there was no point in going any higher until we had made a reconnaissance.

We put the tent down on what was the base camp for the mountain.

CHAPTER IV

At the Basin Rim

PLANNING the expedition, we had bargained for three coolies climbing high with us, and accordingly we had purchased ammunition boots, sleeping bags, and high-altitude clothing for them. Now, to their delight, we extracted this equipment from kitbags. Excepting the sleeping bags it had all been purchased from the Glasgow Barrows, a kind of hawker's paradise in Gallowgate where you can buy at cut-throat prices anything from a wooden leg to a pair of long drawers.

This kit was ex-W.D. stock, and consisted of wind-proof smocks and trousers, felt hats with earflaps, woollen and wind-proof gloves, socks, and, most speculative, the boots. These boots were a pure gamble. We prayed that they would fit. Beaming all over, Sangia, Madbir, and Goria tried them on. They fitted. It was nothing short of miraculous.

We were all set for an attack on Bethartoli. From what Murray had seen, he reckoned the North ridge of our original choice might do if not too avalanche-swept. He had climbed on a corridor, which if it continued above, might see us to the upper part of the mountain. Otherwise we would be exposed to a frightening mass of *séracs* and hanging ice. The alternative was the East ridge, part of which we could see from here. To gain it we would need to climb an 18,000-foot peak, then contour an upper glacier and climb a steep-looking rock step leading to the ridge connecting with the top.

The Dauli is on a trade route to Tibet, a narrow ravine climbing fantastic rock walls
that sweep down from great peaks

On the crest of the Lata Kharak looking across the Dauli to a welter of unclimbed
peaks

The first near view of our mountain Bethartoli Himal, 20,840 feet

The Rishi Gorge, a fierce tangle of rock faces, avalanche debris, hanging jungle, and prickly shrubs

The Rishi Gorge

Crossing the Rishi.   Rope handrails were deemed a wise precaution as anyone falling
into this grinding torrent would almost certainly be killed

McKinnon going across the bridge to fix the handrail

Camp 2, Bethartoli Himal. Behind the ice ridge, soaring over the rock rim of the " Basin ", the peak of Nanda Devi, 25,645 feet

View from Camp 3 on Bethartoli Himal, looking NE. to the spears of the " Basin Rim "

The wonderful peaks of the " Basin Rim ", Changabang and Kalanka in the centre, Rishi Kot to the right, and an unnamed peak extreme right

Homage to Nanda Devi, " The Blessed Goddess "

We set off on reconnaissance of the North ridge, up the corridor. The going was easy, yet below us was the glacier, and towering over us were ice walls surging from our peak above. Up here, crag martins were skimming, and pipits spiralling earthwards in courtship song.

A long look through binoculars and we had made our decision. There was no doubt that this protecting screen continued. The real worry now was the steep step under the summit which had made us ponder since we had first sighted the peak. Now that we were close to it we could see we had not underestimated it. There was nothing like rubbing noses on it. We returned quickly to camp and established Camp 2 without delay.

This was a most beautiful camp, by a running stream in sight of the peaks of the Basin Rim. Towards evening the clouds that had lain on the high tops were lifting, and as the low sun broke through they cleared. Sharper and more inaccessible looking than anything we had ever seen was the 22,000-foot peak of Changabang, a tooth so sheer that its ice could only be a veneer for rock. Dunagiri, Kalanka, Rishi Kot, and an unnamed peak were fit neighbours for this masterpiece in mountain architecture. Very close to us, the long snow ridge of unclimbed Devistan made us long for a decent supply of food to try them. There was an afterglow on the peaks that sent us into our sleeping bags contented. After darkness had fallen a green glow still lingered round the tooth of Changabang and on Bethartoli Himal.

There was snow on the ground when we rose at 5 a.m. The Dhotial does not like snow, and cold demoralizes him. There was little enthusiasm for work this morning, but we got them off by eight o'clock. It was hard going, very hard, for the hillside was a mass of loose stones. Once up this we were able to traverse on snow to the true ridge of the mountain. The route now continued on rock requiring handhold as well as foothold, steep for laden men. Although troubled by altitude the coolies climbed well.

Soon the ridge narrowed to an *arête*, corniced on one side, with a little *gendarme* blocking the way. It was evident we could not take the coolies much further, so Murray stayed here with a rope while we climbed on to see what lay ahead. In a short distance we were stopped by a deep cleft that told its own story. Our height would be just under 18,000 feet, which must be nearly a record for Dhotials climbing on difficult ground. We congratulated them and they departed for the lower camp, eager to get away from this place.

The drop below looked far from reassuring. Further, bad weather which had been brewing all day was closing in fast. On Murray's reappearance it was agreed that he and Scott would look at the obstacle ahead while McKinnon and I would dig camp sites out of the narrow ridge.

They reported with bad news. It was possible to climb down a hundred feet of the impasse, but an out-tilted *gendarme* with another drop of a hundred was a cut-off. To rope down meant no retreat, for it would be impossible to climb back, and there was no escape on the other side.

The only way to get over this nasty shock was to crawl into the tents and get the Primus going to melt snow for pemmican soup and some tea and biscuits. I found eating at this height to be a breathless affair and was glad to desist. A slight feeling of headache showed I was a long way from being acclimatized. We all felt the same way I think, though McKinnon and Scott ate with hearty appetites.

It was cold in the night and sleep in the thin air was difficult. Our breath froze in the tent, but we were reasonably warm in our double sleeping bags. The reward of being up here came in the morning with Nanda Devi shooting skyward over our heads, and round us the fierce peaks of the Basin Rim thrusting their spires to the green sky. Our tents on the narrow ridge looked so tiny, perched high above the glacier and so close to the huge *séracs* above the ice-fall.

Dr. Longstaff had warned us of the speed at which the sun affects Himalayan snow, so we wasted no time in packing up and fixing crampons. A gully below us promised a steep descent of a thousand feet to the easier going of the glacier. This seemed better than scrambling on the ridge with heavy rucksacks.

Murray and I started down. Confidently I planted in my spikes to discover in a short distance that they were balling up, making my footing insecure. Soon I was doing an involuntary glissade, to be brought up on the rope. This method of progress was so superior to kicking or cutting, I took off my crampons and did a standing glissade to a patch of rock. Murray did the same. We then began cutting.

It was a nasty descent, calling for care and incessant step-cutting, gruelling work with heavy sacks. The last two hundred feet was the best of it. We lowered our sacks on the rope, then let go. They shot far out on to the glacier, for this part of the wall was so steep we had to crane our necks to see its foot. We shot after them in a joyous standing glissade. Gathering our stuff together we pushed on down, finding the lower traverse so hard we were glad we had not been born Dhotials. McKinnon and Scott were in camp ten minutes before us, having taken note of our difficulties and followed the lower ridge.

That was Bethartoli. There was no time for another attempt but our failure had taught us a few things about Himalayan climbing, camping at high altitudes, and our reactions to altitude. Further, three of our porters had been initiated into mountaineering and had stood the test well. We had been shown, too, that ridges must not be taken for granted as in the Alps, where invariably one reaches the top that way.

The lesson was to be rubbed in. Rising above the Rishi, the 19,930-foot peak of Hanuman had taken Scott and McKinnon's fancy. They had seen it from their 16,000-foot peak, and we had seen it from another angle

on Bethartoli. Its South-east ridge seen from these two
directions did not look difficult, and although we had
insufficient food for another attempt on Bethartoli, two
days might suffice for Hanuman, for it was on our way
out of the gorge.

For myself, the peak did not attract me. It looked
stony and uninteresting compared with the 19,000-foot
subsidiary peak of Bethartoli on which I had set my heart.
But it was a mountain, and I was only too willing to fall
in with the wishes of the party.

We lost no time in pushing back to the Rishi bridge and
putting a camp up at 16,000 feet on the shoulder of this
peak. The weather was unprepossessing, snow and thick
mist. Cold prevented sleep for a long time.

Next morning we began a long upward slog over a
treacherous boulder-field, to face eventually a series of
steep couloirs between rock ribs, steep for 1000 feet, but
connected to the main ridge. Traversing alternately
between rock and snow we gained its misty crest, and for
1500 feet all was well, until a steep band of rock blocked
the way. Wherever we tried it was difficult. Eventually
Scott made a good lead up it, climbing as though he were
in Glen Coe and not at 19,000 feet on a strange peak.
The last move, a delicate balance on rotten rock, was far
from pleasant.

Above that steep step we had a shock coming to us.
The ridge dropped to a cut-off as on Bethartoli, only this
one was more spectacular, the shifting mist adding considerably to its sheer depth. Above the cleft the ridge
rose steeply to the summit. We abandoned the climb.

In view of the weather, that cleft was perhaps pro-
vidential. The weather had been poor all day, but a
definite deterioration set in as we climbed downwards.
The couloir demanded a lot of care with traverses on
slippery rock, steps to cut in ice, and much steep snow to
descend. Added to that I had a headache and a slight
feeling of sickness.

In fast-falling snow and thick mist we had an anxious time racing the gathering darkness as we steered a compass course for the tents. We were debating our position on an unfamiliar ridge when suddenly, out of the cloud floated the head of Nanda Devi. We sank down to take in this incredible vision, much too far up to be part of the earth, when the moving cloud enveloped it again, leaving us to mist, snow, and gathering darkness.

We turned downhill, acting on the assumption that our line was too high for the camp. Benightment seemed certain, for this boulder-field was a veritable desert, and our chance of hitting the camp in nil visibility was slender. Suddenly Scott shouted he could smell wood smoke. We turned into the wind and found ourselves in camp.

The coolies did us proud. They had not only kept a fire going but hot water was on the boil, and in no time we had soup and tea served to us in our sleeping bags. The wild night that followed made us thankful to be inside, and not out there among the boulders waiting for dawn.

We remember with gratitude the morning of our last high camp in the Rishi. There was no need of an early start, so we could sit outside in the sunshine with every peak of the Nanda Devi basin around us sparkling in new snow. Far below was the Rishi, steep-walled and shadowy, without colour. Up here the rock, snow, and ice was alive, chasing away disappointment for our failure of yesterday. It was the mountains that mattered, not the summits.

Packing up, we kept high as arranged with the base camp party, dropping down one march ahead of the Rishi bridge, thus dodging a difficult bit of country. Our food position was now so bad we were compelled to eat some horrible beans that had been supplied to us in lieu of lentils. They defied cookery. Whether steeped in advance, or boiled for hours, it made no difference to their hard hearts. We ate them mixed with pemmican and suffered inner tortures from excess wind. Luckily we had a little rice, and at this camp there was an abundance of wild rhubarb.

It was my turn to sleep at the door that night and I was grateful.

Like ourselves, the coolies were short of food and glad to be heading back to more lush pastures. They climbed with a will, headed by McKinnon, whose eye for country proved so unerring that he picked up a spoon he had lost on the way in to the gorge. Unfortunately it was a very old spoon, and had broken off from its handle. His improvised spoons ever afterwards would make a story in itself.

Many wild flowers had come to bloom since we passed this way, little forget-me-nots, blue and pink, wild garlic, sweet peas, and hillsides of yellow broom. Over the river we had a new bird in a Himalayan golden eagle, very much like the bird we see on the Scottish hills. Cuckoos were calling too, exactly like the British bird, and it is fairly safe to say they were newly arrived. (The date was 7th June.)

Nanda Devi was veiling and unveiling herself as we dropped through jungle to our camp site below Dibrugheta. Murray's ice axe was a welcome find here, since he thought it had been lost in the gorge. There was regret at leaving Dibrugheta. Its alp was a mass of flowers, and its birches a place for lingering. But we had to cross the ravine and rock climb up the slabs to cross to the snow beds below Dharashi. At 14,000 feet on the pass, a cuckoo landed beside us, a marmot, tiny thing, came out to inspect us, and two large bees flew over the col.

There was little enthusiasm for food. The beans and rhubarb were frightening us with stomach pains and internal rumblings. All of us had diarrhoea. We could not get to Tapoban too quickly.

It was a bad morning for the hardest march across the Lata Kharak. Snow fell till 8 a.m., so that it was 9 a.m. before we got going. Unerringly we found the route, thus the time lost was saved. Further, very little step-cutting was required as most of the snow had melted from the ledges on this side. It was a different story on the other side. We took a high-level route this time, crossing many gullies which called for care.

It was not a pleasant evening, wet and cloudy, with thunder. For me it was enlivened by the sight of three Himalayan thar. These long-haired animals were on a great crag, difficult to see in their door-mat colour. They climbed at amazing speed, their horns showing beautifully against the skyline as they rounded an *arête* steep enough to guarantee a rock climber a climb. At our old camp site we were relieved to find water laid on in a bed of old snow still lingering, and we lost no time in putting down the tent.

The morning was one of the finest we had in India, a spring-like morning, with tree pipits singing and bull-finches calling. Over our still darkened ridge, Bethartoli had the flush of sunrise on its fluted head. In a flood of warmth the sunlight spread to our ridge and filled the valleys with colour. We ate our porridge feeling that this indeed was the height of pure enjoyment.

Behind us was the Rishi. Six thousand feet below us were our thirteen crates of food, but even this bait made us sorry to leave the heights for the fly-ridden haunts of men. We took our last look at Bethartoli. From here we had pronounced our first judgement. Wiser now, we were able to appreciate much that we had been unable to appreciate before.

CHAPTER V

The Dauli

THERE was excitement in Lata when we reappeared. The villagers turned out in welcome, old men, youths, pot-bellied children. I pointed the camera to take a photograph, and at once a mangy cat and an abused-looking jungle crow were produced as assets to the picture. No one seemed to mind the flies which settled on lips and nostrils.

We needed coolies to uplift our stuff from Tapoban, six miles away, to our next group of peaks at the head of the Bagini glacier. Also, in the absence of a fatted calf, we intended to celebrate with the next best thing, a sheep or a goat. Murray opened negotiations for these items. Coolies and a goat would be forthcoming in the evening. Meantime we were invited to occupy the school house eight hundred feet below.

We were disappointed men. The goat failed to arrive, though our coolies were out scanning the hillsides till darkness drove them to bed despondent. And the promised men to shift our crates were like the goat. We were annoyed, but determined not to climb eight hundred feet to reopen negotiations. There was a place marked on the map as Suraithota. It was only three miles away and the boundary of the mysterious Inner Line. Such a place must have coolies.

Murray set off next morning for Suraithota, while we sped down the Dauli to Tapoban and the thirteen crates. Without fuss we were admitted to the bungalow and were soon tucking in to what seemed the feast of a lifetime. Never has simple food tasted better. Our sorrow was that Murray was absent, for he was overdue for a good meal.

By mid-afternoon I was alone. Scott and McKinnon were off in a last bid for the Inner Line Pass. The Holy Shrine of Joshimath boasts a post office, and our final arrangements at Ranikhet had been for all mail to be sent to this village on the Alaknanda Pilgrim Route.

Meantime, Murray was chasing up and down the Dauli valley. Suraithota was a delusion. It was not even a village, just a place marked on the map where there was a Rest House. So he had to climb back to Lata and reopen negotiations. Then, having concluded the deal success-fully, he had another six miles to walk to join me. He was tired and hungry and with pleasure I watched him eat the best meal he had had in three weeks.

Mosquitos and heat prevented sleep that night. By day we were besieged with flies that swarmed on food, face, hands, and anywhere they could settle. We worked in-doors, for both of us had despatches to write for the Press.

The coolies had more interesting work. They were on the track of a goat. It seemed an elusive beast for they had been after it since our arrival in Tapoban twenty-four hours before. Now they led it in for inspection. The goat was a sheep, diseased in the head and smelling abominably. But Sangia grinned broadly and pronounced it " thik ". If it was good enough for this connoisseur it was good enough for us. Its flesh was as tough as it had looked lean in life, but it was good to taste meat again, and eaten with potatoes it seemed a noble dish. On the altruistic side we had done it a service by putting it out of its misery.

The Lata men were expected at 7 a.m., so we were up at five nailing the crates and getting the baggage arranged. They were a well-dressed crew in smart homespuns, young, and anxious not to carry a pound more than the agreed sixty. Loads were picked up and slung down. The spring

D

balance was brought out, and fierce wrangles developed between our own coolies and them. When every man had selected his load, four or five bundles still lay on the ground.

There was enough rejected gear for three men. As we wondered what to do, the offer was made to split it if we would give them wages for three more men. It was a sporting offer, but it meant that some were carrying a hundred pounds. However, we agreed to stop at Lata if they undertook to make a long march on the following day. Agreement reached, we moved off, hoping McKinnon and Scott would catch up on us, for they were long overdue.

It was dark when they came in, overjoyed at locating us and ready for the feast of meat simmering on the fire. An attack of dysentery in Joshimath had laid Scott low, and for twenty-four hours he had had a fearful time, till cured by McKinnon's sulpha drugs. The twelve-mile march to here must have been punishing for him in his weak state.

We cut short their description of Joshimath as a beautifully-situated place riddled with disease, to ask, as sweetly as possible, if there was any mail. Our patience had been sorely tried waiting for it, and eagerly we read the news from home by candlelight. The big item, the arrival of the Inner Line Pass, was treated as unimportant besides the doings of the folks at home. We could proceed with the assurance that we would not be turned back.

When it came to lifting the loads, the Lata wallahs infuriated us by a continuation of yesterday's wrangling. Not knowing the language, one could only stand by and leave it to our coolies. Perimal was a poor substitute for Kuar Singh. He was too good natured and too unsure of himself to be dominating. Sangia stepped into the breach and showed we had made a mistake by not appointing him head coolie, a post he had held before and of which he was well worthy. Although good natured like Perimal, he could rapidly transform himself into a demon, with such drive and energy behind his commands that people automatically obeyed. He gave us a demonstration now, and by 7.30 a.m. we got on the march.

Our way lay up the Dauli valley on the trade route to Tibet by the Niti Pass. We had been impressed with it lower down. This march impressed us a lot more. The rock walls had closed in, relieved only by a few side gorges where trees managed to cling. Otherwise the vertical landscape was the grey of mica. Cut out of the rock, sometimes built out on stanchions, the track threaded its way upwards, poised sometimes above the glacier torrent that rushed between 5000-foot walls in a frightening rumble. None of us had ever imagined such grim ferocity, such unrelenting mountain walls.

Our fellow travellers were as interesting as the scenery. There were Tibetans wearing bush hats and coloured woollen boots below frock coats. Carrying packs they herded large flocks of sheep and goats, each beast fitted with little saddle-bags containing salt and borax. Often the path was thronged with these animals, transporting several tons of cargo. It was astonishing to think they had crossed the Himalaya from Tibet, and would recross when they had bartered their goods for Indian grain and rice.

There were camps of Nomads too, dark-skinned people of low caste who sold us bantam-like eggs at the excessive price of six annas (9*d*.). And well-dressed families in homespuns who were travelling with their animals and all their household gear, to climb high above the tree line and camp on the growth of new grass and flowers springing up as the June snows retreated. All the time there was an upward or downward passage of goats and sheep, donkeys and mules. Some of the women were laden like donkeys, carrying baskets on their arms as well as loads on their backs.

The end of the march was an attractive spot called Juma, where there was a dak bungalow. Looking back the way we had come we saw the cleft in true perspective. The route must be dangerous in the rains or in winter, for the path is exposed, and one could do little to avoid avalanche or stone-fall from above.

We were a happy band at the bungalow. These Lata men were first-class carriers, and they were enjoying themselves. So much so, they asked if they could come with us for the whole trip. As we meant to climb the Bagini peaks and might not require coolies for some time we said " no ". It was reassuring however to know that these coolies were available if the upper Dauli proved a loss.

We left in trailing mists for the climb to Dunagiri. The path wound sensationally, giving the photographers fine opportunities for shots of pack-carrying sheep and goats. Down a scree gully with steep rocks, and we crossed the Dauli to climb up the wall of a ravine. Perched on its slope was an attractive village quite deserted. We wondered why, for the houses were well built on lawn-like turf, and carved wooden balconies ornamented the upper stories.

At this time we did not know that the Bhotia tribes have summer, autumn, and winter homes. Just now, in mid-summer, they were at their highest villages, grazing their flocks on grass new-grown from melted snows. From these advanced villages the men journey far into Tibet, trading, while the women work in the fields or spin cloth or carpets. 3500 feet above us was the Bhotia village of Dunagiri at 11,800 feet. We climbed up to it eagerly.

The change of scene in the short distance was astonishing. Instead of rock, there was a cover of sweet-smelling shrubs, wild roses, walnut. Yet the going was airy, the path being built in places like a bridge, spanning deep crags. At 9000 feet we were in the Alpine zone, familiar little plants and mosses blooming everywhere. In the trees I saw a velvet-cheeked nuthatch.

Soon we were among stone walls and well-tilled fields where hedges grew as in England. At 11,800 feet we entered Dunagiri village, built like a fortress on the hillside. By watching pine grosbeaks, meadow buntings, rufus hedge sparrows, snow pigeons, etc., Scott and I had missed a ceremonious welcome from the village elders. The treat was over, but we made up for it by going on tour.

In front of each group of houses were courtyards in which were assembled the village ladies busy with their looms, or wool spinning. Young and old had jobs to do. Some spread grain to dry in the sun, some worked a dark sticky substance called " pul ", a kind of animal feed. We were much taken by the health and good looks of everyone. The children had rosy cheeks, and we were given happy smiles.

Some of the village maidens were quite beautiful, ornamented with large rings in their noses and more brightly clad than most Himalayan women we had seen. In most villages the women were not only ugly but dressed in drab rags. The men seemed to do nothing but smoke hubble-bubble pipes and dandle children on their knees. It seemed a good life.

Our camp was clear of the village by a stream, an engaging spot giving us a spectacular view at sunset when the Hathi Parbat group came out of the clouds that had enveloped them all day. The Dauli valley was filled with cloud. We looked over this sea to a ragged edge that seemed to hang from the sky. Impossible at first to believe they were mountains. But the trailing vapours moved and the ragged edge stayed still, disappearing in a billow from the Dauli.

We were away at 6 a.m. for a peak marked on the map at 17,830 feet. It meant a 6000-foot climb, but more important than the peak was the northward view we expected to get from it. Reconnaissance from here would tell us something about the unknown Lampak group where we hoped to get a summit. McKinnon was having an off day, and Scott dropped out with a painful tendon. Murray and I continued.

The first 3000 feet was like a Scottish hill, landing us

on a ridge of boulders. We had looked forward to getting to this ridge. We were no sooner on it than we wished we were off it. The whole place was fearfully loose. Fortunately we had the excitement of pinnacles, where route finding was tricky. We climbed unroped and moved with care. Once we tried a traverse to avoid a pinnacle at a high angle, but a stone-fall took place over the very ground we would have crossed. We retired and climbed the pinnacle, handling it like delicate china.

We were in clouds now, but climbed onwards, over heart-breaking shale, then on to snow, then over another little pinnacle, to find a snow dome which was the summit. The peak had taken seven and a half hours. Without very much hope we waited for a view before being driven down by cold.

Descent was unpleasant. Every step had to be watched and each boulder selected for stability. We felt as skittish as goats once on the grass, and fairly raced down. After our weakness on Bethartoli and Hanuman it was a relief to feel an energy that showed we were acclimatized. Although we had seen nothing of reconnaissance value we did not feel our day wasted.

McKinnon had not wasted his day either. He had opened a dispensary in Dunagiri and done good work. There was more sickness than we supposed, the worst case being a little girl with a gangrenous foot. The foot was rotten with pus and the toes were shapeless. He had cleaned it thoroughly and treated it with penicillin, but had little hope of a cure. As reward he had been given a bag of potatoes, Scottish potatoes, which was the main-crop of Dunagiri. These potatoes were the finest any of us had ever eaten. They had been introduced to this village by a far-seeing agricultural department. At this altitude they took an hour to cook.

For the first hour or two of our climb, until about 8 a.m., the weather had been clear enough to get good views of the high peaks of the Bagini glacier and the Hathi

Parbat group. Given a sufficiently early start it might be possible to climb a 16,600-foot peak above the camp to arrive in time for a view. Scott and McKinnon were all for the idea, and while we lay in bed, they rose at 2 a.m.

Down in camp it cleared to a glorious morning, and I had an amusing time visiting the village school and turning things out of my pockets for their enjoyment. The schoolmaster was a thin-faced autocrat dominating a court-yard full of children from about five to eight years of age. On production of my pocket compass he promptly gave them a lecture on the mariner's compass. They were intelligent lively children, squatting on little mats, with slates and jars of liquid chalk. Their books were of the simplest kind, containing line drawings of objects with the Hindustani word in large letters under it. Down by the stream women were washing in primitive tubs hollowed out of tree trunks.

The big event in Dunagiri was the building of a new schoolhouse. It was sited below our camp, and all that morning there was a great rumbling of boulders as stones were slid down to the site for breaking. The stone-breakers shaped them, and an official with a blue-print supervised the laying. Although no one seemed to be working very hard it was taking shape at quite a speed.

At half-past one McKinnon and Scott appeared, full of enthusiasm for a wonderful climb. They had seen nothing of value, but had found a rock *arête* which began low on the peak and provided a granite edge of magnificent sound-ness almost to the top. Further, they had found the father and mother of all glissades, which took them down 3000 feet of steep snow on their bottoms. Murray and I looked at each other and arranged an early start. We might get the reconnaissance yet.

Nobly the coolies lit a fire, made chapatties and saw us on our way. This at 2 a.m. in a smirr of rain with flicker-ings of lightning in the sky. In darkness we fumbled through scrub, and I had to halt frequently with diarrhoea.

By daybreak we were happy to see a change for the better. The clouds were still down on the peaks but their general level was higher.

We climbed up to our right and found the *arête*. It was as they said, clean and sound, and we came to life in the most enjoyable bit of mountaineering we were to find in India. It was like an Alpine ridge, not difficult in the main, but airy, with one rather awkward section. The clouds welling up around us in the still air gave a wonderful feeling to the place. We caught glimpses of mountain walls thousands of feet above us, and valley floors thousands of feet below us. Once our shadows were thrown on a circle of rainbow in what is known as the Brocken Spectre.

On top we were enshrouded, but waited hopefully for a clearing. Our reconnaissance was not in vain. There was a quick shifting of clouds and we had a fragmentary view of sharp peaks piercing the clouds. They shone like silver spears, steep and uncompromising looking. Beyond doubt they were the peaks we hoped to climb. But even in the short time they were before us they gave no cause for optimism. We would require to look from their other side to see if there was an easier approach.

There was no trouble finding the glissade. Eight hundred feet of boulders and we struck the snowy corrie. We were off with a rush in an exhilarating slide that seemed to go on for ever. This was indeed a de-luxe mountain. Back in camp at 12.15 p.m. we felt we had made two days out of one.

McKinnon reported a miraculous transformation in his patient. The leg which had seemed beyond hope was well on the mend, and would recover if the treatment were continued. This was indeed good news. The mother had been instructed what to do, likewise the schoolmaster, who was a man of intelligence and responsibility.

We held a council of war. In view of what we had glimpsed, the Bagini glacier seemed out of question. To

Camp at 16,000 feet on Hanuman ; clouds fill the Rishi Gorge

Pack-carrying goats in the Dauli Valley.   Each of these beasts carries a load of 24 lb.

The deserted village of Ruing on the Dauli

A young woman and child and an old crone of Dunagiri

This eligible girl has an ov
size in nose rings, not
mention bears' claws, sil
shoulder strap, and elega
necklaces

Dunagiri schoolchildren
their work at 11,800 fee
The schoolmaster seat
cross-legged was very mu
the "master" here

unagiri Bhotias.   These
hotias of the Tibet border
re themselves half-Tibetan

hese little girls have un-
    usual caste marks

Loading the jopa, a jo
requiring strong teeth

These animals are crosse
between yak and cow

This rather handsome
" jopa-wallah " prepares hi
chapatties

Approaching Malari village up the Dauli with our jopa train

This little girl of Malari is beyond the scope of the expedition's " Health Service ". Malformation of the limbs and anaemia seemed to be the trouble

Lampak base camp. Scott shows off some of Goria's exquisite chapatties whil McKinnon and Sangia look on

The north face of Tirsuli, 23,210 feet above the Uja Tirche glacier

move to the other side of the range meant crossing three high passes to gain a position on the Siruanch glacier in the middle of a horseshoe of 20,000-foot peaks. It promised not only a wonderfully-situated base camp, but was the first step towards solution of a problem that had intrigued us since we first made plans for the Himalaya, the problem of getting from the Dauliganga to the Goriganga by the Girthi Gorges, of which nothing was known.

Solution would have more than academic interest for us. It would take us in a direct line from west to east, instead of retracing our steps and detouring by the usual northward route, a route described by Dr. Longstaff as tedious and bleak.

With this alluring prospect before us we took stock of our food. As Minister of Food I had imposed no rationing of any kind, save in the Rishi when conservation had been necessary owing to the unexpected loss of flour. The stocktaking showed we were going just a little heavily on items like butter, cheese, honey, and jam. Apart from a small camp ration to give variety to the chapatties, biscuits would have to be reserved for high camps.

All of us had good appetites and seemed to be enjoying food. Breakfast at this time consisted of porridge with sugar and milk, followed by scrambled egg and chapatties. The chapatties were thin, like crumpets, tasty when eaten hot. We usually had about six per man, that quota to include the allocation for the march.

The main meal was invariably soup, made from Maggi dried powder, a Swiss soup known to mountaineers the world over. Into it we put pemmican, adding onions, lentils, and rice. I liked mine on the thin side, but the others liked theirs thick, in the form of a " hoosh ". The fine Scottish potatoes here were a boon and we whaled into them. No wonder the people of this place were healthy. It was about this time I cut up my old pyjamas to use for experiments with steamed puddings. Until then, rice and wild rhubarb had been our standby.

Murray was horrified when he saw me lift my string-tied bundle out of the pot.   It was a waste of good flour, raisins, and suet.   Whoever heard of dropping a pudding into boiling water ?   The stuff would be saturated.   Without waiting to see it, he advised throwing it away.   My heart sank, for he is not a man of hasty judgement.

I might have thrown it away, but Scott and McKinnon had their spoons raised and an eager look in their eyes. Unwrapped, it looked a neat little pudding, khaki-coloured and quite dry.   Murray not only ate his words, he ate the pudding, and asked for more.   The steamed-pudding era had been ushered in.

CHAPTER VI

To Malari

NOW that we had decided to move, the question upper-most in our minds was coolies. We weighed the baggage to estimate the number required and went down to inter-view the headman. He had promised us coolies. It now appeared we were to have jopas, and not coolies. We did not know what jopas were, but assumed it was the Hindu name for the fine horses we could see grazing around us. Each beast would carry a hundred and sixty pounds, we were told. They would be forthcoming in the morning.

Meantime we examined the first pass with critical eyes. It rose as a fearsomely steep grass slope. Climbing it with hundred-and-sixty pound loads was going to give us a display of horse-power. Except that the jopas were not horses, but enormous, horned animals, with the ponderous step of a rhinoceros. They were crosses between yak and cow.

Our loads were sorted out into neat, two-maund parcels, each parcel being a jopa load. Like Kuar Singh at Garur, the jopa wallah had other ideas. Seizing two small bundles he pursued the nearest jopa and tied this load on it. When each beast had its load there was still a fair amount of baggage strewn about the ground. We remonstrated.

At once there was disorder. Yesterday's agreement was forgotten. The jopas were carrying all they could carry. The jopa wallah was a liverish individual who swept aside all objections. Our coolies nearly came to blows with him, then sorrowfully began picking up the abandoned loads.

It was then the sahibs took a hand. We waved the coolies aside. The jopas would carry all the baggage or none at all. In a rage the jopa wallah gathered together his beasts and slung off our luggage. We could go to hell.

Murray, our spokesman, took the situation calmly. The jopa wallah had washed his hands of us. Very well, we would wash our hands of him, and at the same time, report this affair to the village headman. At once there was a change of front. Hands were folded in respect, negotiations reopened, and eventually we moved off, the beasts carrying their two-maund loads at the old rate of pay.

The climb to the foot of the pass was joyful with the songs of Himalayan rubythroats and skylarks. On the steep ascent we began to get anxious for the jopas. Their liverish owner had left them in charge of two herdsmen, and they seemed to be fighting a losing battle in getting them uphill, for the beasts wanted to go down, not up. Chasing up and down, making grunting sounds, whistling, slapping, they got them to the crest at 13,620 feet.

Below us, in contrast to the surrounding peaks of grey stone, we were agreeably surprised to find a verdant corrie where bubbling springs wound amongst flowers. The air was warm and pleasant, and even the overloaded jopas seemed to enjoy the descent. We negotiated a ford over a rather difficult glacier stream and camped among stones.

There was no view of the peaks, but the pass above looked abominably steep. The jopa drovers shook their heads and wrangled with the coolies. We did not intend to reopen that old argument. The thing settled itself next day in the misty steeps of a rocky corrie with the quaking beasts at the point of collapse. Reaching the top at 14,790 feet, our coolies descended to lighten the troubled jopas, returning with the jubilant drovers who danced round us shaking hands. Their beasts had made it, and we had helped them out. Gleefully they slapped the sides of their sweating animals.

Here, in the clouds, we met our first Malari wallah, a quaintly dressed Bhotia wearing finely woven homespuns in a kind of flannel skirt over long white pants of similar material. He smoked a hubble-bubble which quickly went the rounds of our men. His pleasant smile and kindly face took our fancy and we plied him with questions. Was there a route through the Girthi? Could we get coolies at Malari? Was there food available in the village? To all our questions he smiled an affirmative. And to substantiate his claims he appointed himself coolie forthwith, abandoning his own plans to take on the post of assistant jopa wallah. This was obviously a man who knew his mind, for he had been intent on crossing the pass in the opposite direction until he met us.

Once below the cloud we saw we were in a different kind of country. Bare slopes of sparse grass, red screes, crumbly rock towers devoid of vegetation, gave a Tibetan aridity to the scene. Far below us was the grey Dauli, its gorge walls still unrelenting. Dropping steadily we reached the floor of the corrie where little walls were built round brown fields parched for lack of rain.

Malari village when it came into view was startling for its ugliness and grim situation, a town of houses clinging to a drab hillside on the edge of a ravine. Many of its buildings appeared overdue to fall into its depths, erosion by landslide and rain having cut close to their foundations. The arable ground below the village had the mica look of the Dauli, dusty and parched.

To our joy, there was a neat little dak bungalow. But it was not for us apparently. First of all the Chowkidar demanded a pass, then told us the key was kept in Joshi-math. None of us believed this to be true, but we did not intend to argue. There was a place for camping and we promptly unloaded the tent. At once the padlock was wrenched off the door and we were invited to enter. As

TO MALARI AND THE LAMPAK MOUNTAINS

Dr. Longstaff says, " Never worry about a situation till you meet it." This young Chowkidar was merely trying to be awkward, and we had called his bluff.

The village was a motley of rubbage dumps, ruins, and well-built houses with fine carvings. There was no shyness about the ladies here, but quite a lot of filth. They lacked the clean, healthy look of the Dunagiri girls. Round a carved wooden frame on what we took to be the village square, were grouped the elders, and some not so old, many with babies on their knees. By the time I had taken a photograph, half the village was present, most of them following at my heels everywhere I went. A full fifty accompanied me back to camp, trooping behind as though I were king of the procession.

Murray had, more wisely, kept his mind on business. Ata, the native flour, and tsampa, a kind of roasted grain we used in lieu of porridge, were the main items required. We needed sufficient for a full five weeks, to give us three weeks' climbing on the Lampak mountains, then the traverse of the Girthi Gorges. The gorges were known to the Malari men apparently, and some of them were prepared to see us through.

Next day was a busy one. Scott and McKinnon made off to Bampa Post Office, the last place for mail this side of Tibet. Two memsahibs of the World-Wide Evangelization Crusade reported to be working there put new life into their steps and they disappeared in a cloud of dust. Murray and I had writing to do, ata to weigh, and baggage to sort out.

To our astonishment, after helping us to get the gear in order, our Malari wallahs broke their agreement by demanding more wages, stipulating at the same time that loads would need to come down from fifty to forty pounds. Evening saw us without coolies, our six faithful Dhotials excepted. We refused to kow-tow to them, but intended scouring the country for fresh coolies, since we did not intend to be victimized by their unreasonable demands. We did not want it to be said that any Bhotia ever put one over a Glasgow man.

The head coolie was the trouble maker. Even his moustache contrived to look sullen. At seven next morning he repeated his offer to Perimal, our Dhotial chief; but we said nothing, we merely swung on our rucksacks. Eyebrows were raised. Where were we going? We were going to look for coolies, even if it meant going back the length of the Dauli to Joshimath. We were prepared to pay a reasonable sum, not the unreasonable figure demanded for two short marches carrying only forty pounds.

This ultimatum had an immediate effect. The Malari wallahs saw they were about to lose a job. They babbled to their headman, and he, seeing he was outnumbered, swung round to our way of thought. We were back

where we started. They would come with us at the
old rates.

By evening there was another impasse. Only twelve
coolies were available, but goats could be supplied at no
additional cost. Soon the work of morning was being
undone as kitbags were unloaded and the grain transferred
into little saddle-bags, making a twenty-four-pound load
for each animal.

Up in the village there was excitement. Drums were
beating and ritual dancing was in progress. The rains
that would bring life to this parched land were being
celebrated in advance. McKinnon and Scott had assembled
with the whole village to see picked dancers work themselves into an ecstasy before a little altar.

With swigs at a bottle, the lifting and crumbling of
earth through their fingers, bowing before burning incense,
the excitement had reached a terrific climax to a crescendo
of beating drums.

We had missed a treat. The monsoon dance was over
by the time we had crossed the river and climbed to the
village square. For once we could wander by ourselves,
for the celebrations had worn the curiosity out of the most
inquisitive. There was fine carving on the houses, and
the great wood slates of the roofs bore testimony to the
time when wood grew close to the village.

CHAPTER VII

Success

WE left Malari with a queer convoy, nineteen coolies, one cow, and a mixed flock of sheep and goats to the number of eighteen, each animal carrying its twenty-four-pound quota of rice, lentils, flour, and tsampa.

Mounting steeply we were in an exciting country for birds. There were Himalayan greenfinches, vividly patterned birds, slimmer than the British bird and flashed with much more yellow and black ; the red and grey of a wall creeper as it alighted like a nuthatch on rock, showing its square tail and slender curved beak as it climbed; chukor partridge, strongly marked with black bars on lavender ; flocks of brownish mountain finches, the scarlet of rose finches, squeaking sounds of black tits, and the sight of a strange grey and yellow warbler. Higher up, golden eagles circled over us.

Three thousand feet of climbing from Malari, and we camped on a steeply tilted alp. Such a short distance could hardly be called a march. Nor had the camp site the amenities of wood or water to recommend it. But the Malari wallahs wanted to camp and we did not wish to antagonize them by protesting. Their camp strategy was simple. The youngest coolies were given kitbags and told to climb up to the nearest snow beds and bring back some snow. From somewhere they produced yak and cow dung which smouldered dimly but boiled the kettle for all that.

It was an inspiring situation, dramatic with shifting

cloud winding among the rock towers high above the dark walls of the Dauli. Amongst our feet were clumps of flowers, white rose root and anemones being the most beautiful. Immediately behind us the 19,000-foot peak of Kunti Bhannar rose in pinnacles to snow. Tomorrow we would cross its ridge to contour into Lampak.

We were away sharp in the morning, climbing along a ridge that rose to 15,600 feet. With excitement we dropped over the other side. Straight ahead was the Girthi. The Rishi Gorge looked tame by comparison with this rock fastness. The walls seemed to rise sheer to summits fantastically ragged. Then we saw Uja Tirche. It rose above the boil of monsoon clouds, a narrow summit rising thousands of feet above the Girthi in rock bands and ice bulges. Even as we looked the clouds shifted, disclosing twin sickles of ice fringing the cliffs, sweeping down to rock splinters, pinnacles which we knew must be of great size to show from here.

What excited us was the possibility of climbing this peak. It looked difficult, promised mountaineering of the highest order, and the height of 20,350 feet made it a worthy peak. We camped that afternoon on the stones of its glacier, marvelling at our situation close to a great waterfall in the midst of a horse-shoe of unclimbed mountains, the same mountains we had seen from Dunagiri and the camp site exactly as planned.

The Malari men had done well. We were all friends now, even the headman's sullen look had given way to positive enjoyment. Goats unloaded and saddle-bags neatly piled, they lit a fire for us before departing, assuring us that they would return in three weeks' time for the traverse of the Girthi.

We lost no time in sorting out three days' food supply for an attack on Uja Tirche. We had enough food for three weeks' climbing, and ten unclimbed Himalayan giants were ringed round us. We were fit, and the weather at last seemed to be on the uptake.

Morning saw us climbing upwards with six of the coolies. It was a delightful approach, first by a traverse over flower-covered meadows, then by a steep grass slope to a snowy corrie. The coolies were making heavy weather of it, however, and were spread out over 2000 feet of hillside, more often sitting down than carrying on.

I took my own line on the left flank of the corrie, sliding on abominable scree to reach a little peak on the spur of Uja Tirche which promised a view into the unknown country beyond, to Tibet. Behind the camp we had left, clouds were piling up, breaking open now and then to reveal 7000-foot ice walls, fragments of summit ridge, and sharp pointed tops suspended in space.

Suddenly I was on the ridge looking into the other world of Tibet. It was indeed another world, a world roofed by the clearest sky I have ever seen, a sky of pale brittle blue. And rolling away to infinity, range after range of autumn-coloured hills, vegetationless snow-streaked hills, curiously reminiscent of Scotland, particularly of the view south from Cairn Toul in late March when spring has stripped all but the last snowfields from the hillsides. This was the desert of Tibet, a contrast indeed to the snow peaks and the green-clad Himalaya on our side of the watershed.

My peaklet marked the true dividing line between the wet and dry zones, its western face falling sheer as far down as I could see on the Tibet side. The disintegrating nature of the ridge had me worried as I traversed across it. If the pinnacles of Uja Tirche—now in cloud—were a continuation of this ridge as I suspected, then we could look out for sparks, for I had never climbed on rock that needed more delicate handling. Herds of bharral, the wild mountain sheep, stood on the snow gully connecting my ridge with the right arm of the corrie. Gratefully I joined it.

I sat up here to await the others. Scott appeared with bad news. The coolies were going badly. One was sick,

and all of them were feeling the altitude. The rattle of
scree sounded above us and Tom McKinnon appeared out
of the clouds. He had been up amongst the pinnacles and
described them as the craziest things imaginable, but he
had cairned a route until stopped by a great Sphinx head,
fully two hundred feet high and obviously difficult.

Even as we talked, Bill Murray and two of the coolies
appeared. Heroically the coolies returned for the abandoned loads while we built tent platforms from the stones.
Our height would be about 17,400 feet and we felt more
energetic than in previous high camps. The reward of
being up here came at sunset when the enveloping clouds
wreathed upwards and peak after peak stood clear, pink-
shafted above cloud-filled valleys where night had already
fallen.

Breakfast in a high camp is not a jolly affair. Getting
out of the sleeping bag is not so bad as the business which
precedes it, forcing biscuits and lukewarm tea down one's
throat, the latter from a flask filled the night before.
Boots and other preparations seem a confounded nuisance
at such times, and it is a brave man who will say anything
controversial. At 5.30 a.m. with this behind us we set
off on two ropes for the pinnacles, Tom McKinnon and
myself on one, Bill Murray and Douglas Scott on the other.

The pinnacles were indeed a weird sight, towering out
of the clouds, tottering spires, " Old Man of Hoy " shapes,
" Storr Rock " forms, and the Sphinx head which marked
the end of McKinnon's valuable recce. A cap sitting on
top of its head gave it personality, a Sphinx with the
lid on.

McKinnon lost no time in descending to its west face,
where he had detected two wide cracks rising one above
the other, the top one banked with snow, but offering the
possibility of ascent if frozen enough to permit cutting of
hand- and foot-hold. Like the west face of my little
peaklet of the previous day, the situation was exposed.

It was a good choice of route. The first crack went

easily, and there was a hitch for the rope to safeguard the leader on the upper section. I joined him, and we forced the final part of the climb by a combination of step-cutting on the hard-frozen snow-ice, and using hand-holds on the edge of the rock wall. We beckoned on the others and looked round the corner.

The way ahead looked feasible, but involved us in much up-and-down work on rotten rock, till at last we were at the bottle-green ice of the couloir, virtually part of a hanging glacier which we knew marked the beginning of the ice ridge. We retraced our steps to a steep rock chimney, climbed it, and marked the spot with a cairn, climbed over some easy rocks and found ourselves on the ice ridge.

With glee we noted that the snow was hard, suitable for ice claws, so we laced the ten-point spikes on to our boots and started up the *arête*. The spikes gripped beautifully, saving us the job of step-cutting, and we made height quickly. The altitude would be about 18,000 feet and thick mist enshrouded us.

The *arête* was an exciting place, with the west cornice overhanging space and the east eave falling away steeply to —we knew—crags and hanging glacier. The need to take a breath at each step indicated that the ridge was steepening, and a rift in the mist confirmed this. We were below a point where the narrow sickle of the *arête* swept upward to join with the vertical handle of the second sickle. There was no direct ascent. We must traverse across the ice wall to join another *arête* on the right, which made a wedge with the upper part of the ridge. It was corniced on the far side and the angle looked high, but it did not look impossible.

McKinnon led across. At such times it is reassuring to have a good anchorage on the mountain, such as a well-driven ice axe with a turn of rope round it. A slip by the leader can then be checked by the second man. In this case, a few inches of axe-head had to suffice. It looked insufficient with a drop below of thousands of feet. But if it could be climbed I felt sure McKinnon would do it, and if it could not, then I had enough faith in him as a mountaineer to know he would return.

Nevertheless, I speculated on what action I would take should a slip occur. A fall would end in a pendulum swing sixty feet below me. The jerk would be gradual since his main weight would be taken by the inclined wall. I positioned the axe head the best way to take such a shock should it occur.

Cutting hand- and foot-holds he moved across the wall, stopping half-way across to ask me if I was quite happy. He told me he was fairly enjoying himself. Forty feet outward and he swung himself out of sight over the cornice on the far side. Five minutes passed and I heard his cheery cry to " come on ".

The traverse was not easy, extremely awkward in its last move over the bulge of the projecting cornice. Round the corner I found Tom poised on an excessively steep slope with the same kind of belay as I had had myself, a few inches of axe-head in the ice. Some sharp step-cutting and we were on the easier crest of the ridge, but we could see ahead of us a replica of the thing we had climbed, but with a larger section of ice wall to cross.

We did not feel dismayed, neither could I say enthusiastic. Our main feeling was one of astonishment, that we had been able to rise to such a standard of difficulty at this altitude, and hardly notice it during the excitement of climbing. The time factor was our chief worry. We had been going seven hours and the summit was by no means within grasp yet. Interesting too, that at this height of 19,000 feet we needed two breaths to each step on easy ground where it was simply a question of putting one foot carefully in front of the other.

The second ice wall went as the first, but this time we climbed it united as a party of four, to gain the advantage of additional anchorage. Above that the *arête* seemed to go on and on, till suddenly a thin snow blade loomed ahead, the summit.

It was snowing as we crowded on to its narrow top, to look down ice walls disappearing into gloom. In such a situation one does not feel a conqueror, quite the reverse. The climb had taken eight and a half hours, and, apart from it being too cold to linger, we were going to need all our time for the descent. Five minutes up there and we were off.

It was a treacherous descent. The thin snow surface had deteriorated, causing the ice claws to gather a slippery sole which slid on the underlying ice. We took them off and used a different technique. McKinnon was sheet anchor, and he stood firm while Murray led downward to be followed by Scott and myself. Then we dug in till joined by McKinnon. In this way the party were always anchored, and a slip, whether from above or below, could always be checked.

The first ice wall went well, though a certain amount of rope engineering was called into play to safeguard the last man. It was a different story with the second step. The dangers of this traverse were all too apparent, not least being the lack of safe anchorage to protect the leader and save the others from being pulled off in the event of a slip.

We cast around for an alternative, deciding to follow the slope downwards to where it became a rock buttress. Solid footing on the rocks to give safety to the party was what we wanted. We got it after a few hundred feet of excessively steep descent. Two hundred feet of ice wall separated us from our ridge.

We took turns at cutting a passage, McKinnon first, then Murray, then Scott and myself, then Murray again. It was an uneasy crossing, the ice watery and unreliable, difficult by its splintery nature to shape into steps with the ice axe. McKinnon tried ice claws on it and was shot down forty feet to be stopped by the rope when a step broke under his stamp.   Our safety-first tactics had not been in vain.

But around us a minor miracle was taking place.   The mists which had enveloped us all day were submerging to the valleys, making us forget the shivering cold.   In waves of movement peaks were breaking through, Kamet signposting the Badrinath range in a great wedge of silhouette, immense against fire-tinted clouds.   Even as we looked, the warmth was withdrawn from the sky and the cloud sea paled to shadow.   The immensity of depth, of incredible space, is something I am never likely to forget.   It was a feeling of being not on earth, but on another planet.

Meantime, at the end of two hundred feet of climbing rope, Murray was fighting his last battle with the gap. It was a fine piece of mountaineering.   Picking steadily, cutting hand- and foot-holds, he had worked harder than any of us on this traverse, and a triumphant shout told us he was across.   Fastening rope slings to the stretched rope we crossed in his steps.   The method was unorthodox, but was the only one practicable with all our available rope out.   We gained the ridge in moonlight.   The Providence that looks after drunken men and mountaineers had not only submerged the clouds, but had given us a clear sky from which a three-quarter moon shone silvery.

Mentally we had prepared ourselves for a night out on the mountain, thinking we should need to squat down on the first suitable place.   Thanks to the moon we revised our ideas.   Further, our safety was greater since a frost crust was rapidly binding the *arête*, giving certain foot-hold.   It was a wonderful moment when we stepped off the ice on to the rocks of the pinnacle traverse.

Here McKinnon came into his own.   Quickly he found our cairn marking the first chimney—now glazed with ice and calling for care—and we were soon on the route of the morning.   It seemed fearfully hard work, sliding on stones, climbing and contouring among these queer moonlit

The pinnacle ridge on Uja Tirche, 20,350 feet. Climbers near the base of the
central pinnacle

Two peaks are prominently shown

The camp on Uja Tirche. Kamet, 24,477 feet, stands high above the Badrinath peaks

Pinnacles of Uja Tirche. Note the two small figures on the right

Camp on Uja Tirche, looking into Tibet

Camp on Uja Tirche where the dividing line between India and Tibet is cut immediately below the tents by the sheer sides of the Girthi Gorges, at present in cloud

South Lampak peak from the Camp on Uja Tirche. Our attempt went by the left-hand ridge

The view from Camp 3 at 17,800 feet on South Lampak

Madbir and Nurbir had to forage far to keep the base camp at Lampak in fuel, but accepted this task with a smile

Taking advantage of an off day to make pancakes. The author, at the frying pan, is closely watched by coolies

Bhotias and pack-laden goats crossing over the shoulder of Uja Tirche to contour into the Girthi Gorges. "This morning the Himalayas of imagination had come to life. A dark blue, almost black sky, and thrown against it, the peaks that had been our companions for three weeks"

shapes, with the worry of the Sphinx at the back of our minds. This descent went surprisingly well, McKinnon coming down last man, safeguarding us all from above and descending himself unaided. A few complications traversing right and left, and we passed the last pinnacle nine hours after leaving the summit. We reached the tent just eighteen hours after leaving it.

Curiously, no one was hungry, despite having eaten almost nothing on the mountain. Dutifully the coolies had kept a fire going and they were soon out of the tent bringing the kettle to the boil for tea and soup. Our one desire was sleep, but we ate, knowing our bodies needed something after such a strenuous day.

That was Uja Tirche. Looking back on it, I remember no other mountaineering day to equal it for suspense and sustained interest. It was a climb I enjoyed, while remembering the slog of the last few hundred feet to the summit, and the weary climb back over the pinnacles.

Even the camp was a delightful place, perched on the Tibet border and commanding the sunrise and sunset, when at dawn the desert of Tibet was flooded in seas of warm colour, or in the evening when Tirsuli and the ring of 20,000-foot peaks above the Uja Tirche glacier were suffused in Alpine-glow.

CHAPTER VIII

Failure

THE Base Camp seemed a veritable haven after the austere heights, a place for sloth, and we all felt like it. I even had a wash, the first for over a week, this ceremony in honour of some baking by which I proposed to celebrate the ascent of Uja Tirche.

Bampa had not proved a forlorn hope to Scott and McKinnon. The two missionaries, as well as being fine ladies, were excellent cooks, and McKinnon had noted their recipes for biscuits, pancakes, and scones, all made from ata, the local flour.

My attempt at biscuits and scones had not been successful. Some vital detail had been omitted by the Lady's men. But the pancakes were one hundred per cent. I called for my henchman, Goria, and said confidingly, " Bampa memsahib chapattie." His answering " Thik ", carried a wealth of meaning. He returned with a large tin plate, a bag of ata, and a fish-slice made from the lid of a biscuit tin.

The sugar, butter, egg, duly mixed by me, he sprinkled in the flour, giving me knowing grins from time to time. Correctly dispensed, he carried the mixture to the fire. The pan was placed over the flames while I sat with the butter. Operation pancake was in progress, eagerly watched by the other five coolies, each of whom was eager to show Goria how much more efficiently they could turn a pancake. If I dropped in an over-large piece of butter there would be concerted cries of " Bus " (enough). The last pancake to be dispensed was Goria's, a pancake that grew bigger and bigger as the expedition progressed.

Whether making puddings or the ordinary fare of the day, I had only to give Goria a clue and he brought the right stuff. We had our jargon. The big cooking pot was the " bara wallah ". The medium-sized one was the " chota wallah ", and the very small one was the " chota, chota, wallah ". If one wanted the lid for the big pot one simply asked for the " bara topi ". My language was a mixture of Hindustani, Nepali, Bhotia dialect, and Glasgow, but it did the trick, and before the end of the expedition I could carry on quite involved conversations with the men.

They were grand lads who fetched water, hunted the hillsides for firewood, helped us to cook, mended our clothes, and who were prepared to climb themselves to a standstill in our service. Such men could not be treated as pack-horses, or drudges, they were friends with whom we were glad to share a camp fire or even try a vile native cigarette of companionship. Right now they proposed to have a private celebration by killing a goat.

Altogether, our off day was a big success, but the weather gave less cause for satisfaction. From Uja Tirche we had seen a likely mountain to the south of the main Lampak peak. If we could find it, and examine its doubtful parts, we might pronounce judgement. Murray and Scott set off to look for it while McKinnon and myself sorted out a six-day supply of food. Round the fire a butcher's shop had been set up as the coolies cut up a sheep that had been slaughtered in the early hours. The warm liver was presented to us.

Despite low mists and unsettled conditions the recce had not been abortive. Up the glacier was a fine camping spot, believed to be at the foot of this South Lampak peak. We could lose nothing by moving to it, and it would take us into the centre of the horse-shoe.

Scott and McKinnon left in the grey hours next morning while Murray and I followed with the coolies. The stony going seemed very laborious, mutton lassitude affecting us all on the 1500-foot slippery climb. The only suspicious section was where a hanging glacier suspended its ice ready to bombard our route. It proved to be perfectly safe.

The camp spot was an oasis above a rock wall, grassy and so massed with alpine flowers that we had to tramp them down to spread the groundsheet. The great peaks that ringed us round were in cloud, but McKinnon and Scott on their early pilgrimage had glimpsed the ridge above. What little they had seen did not look promising. Further reconnaissance was called for, before we could press upward with the camp.

After a wet night, mild for 15,000 feet, morning was a revelation. Where yesterday there had been seething black cloud behind the tent, the astonishing peak of Tirsuli now stood clear, 8000 feet of ice curtain twisting over crags, hanging from three miles of summit flutings in a glaciated tangle. If there is a route from here to the top of this 23,210-foot peak—the greatest prize left in this part of the world—it will tax the skill and resource of the strongest party.

We lost no time in pushing upwards. The *arête* that had looked uncompromising proved to be quite simple, becoming shale and scree after 2000 feet. Above that, the route continued on snow and broken ground for fully 1000 feet, then rose to a rock buttress. There was no need to go further. Undoubtedly we could place a camp at 18,000 feet or higher.

The fine spell was short lived. Mist was creeping round the fire by mid-afternoon, chilling the air and driving us into the tent.

Morning saw us on the upward climb in low clouds. It was unrelenting work for the coolies, particularly on the upper sections where steps had to be cut in ice and boulders slid away underfoot. Near the rock buttress where the climbing became difficult they indicated that they did not wish to go further. As the weather was deteriorating rapidly with fast falling snow and a thickening mist, it was a good move. We said our " salaams " on the understanding that they would return in two days' time.

Shouldering the packs we climbed onward, to a snow cornice a short distance above. It was the best camping place we had seen on the mountain, sheltered from avalanches and out of range of stones fired from the rock buttress above. The situation was airy with long drops on both sides, but as soon as we were sure it was safe, we dug platforms for the tents and were soon inside, out of the nil visibility and falling snow.

Towards evening our spirits rose again. The clouds broke in the north, rolling along the valleys and showing us the Tibetan peaks, whose tops were about level with our height of over 18,000 feet. Above us, our peak was clear, looking very close, its cornice twisting at quite an easy angle to the top we hoped to tread tomorrow. With high hopes we retired to the sleeping-bag, ready for a 3.30 a.m. rise.

Snow pattering against the tent put paid to any hope of an immediate start. We postponed departure hour by hour, but still the wet snow shook the tent canvas, melted on the outside, percolated to the inside, and formed puddles on the floor. Fortunately we had hip-length mattresses which kept the main part of our bodies from contact with the water. And though my sleeping-bag was sodden from the knees down, and Scott's was in much the same state, we were confident that we would manage to weather it out for yet another day, when we hoped to recce the rock buttress and perhaps try the top.

It seemed to me a long day, with no books to read, unable to sleep, and rationed to a modicum of food. Not that there was much pleasure in eating, but it helped to pass the weary hours and prevent morbid thoughts. At such times the idea of stepping over the snow cornice to eternity seems quite a good way of solving the problem, prevented fortunately by the effort of getting out of a warm sleeping bag into a world of wet snow. All night long avalanches fell on both sides of us.

At 3.30 next morning the snow was still falling, ruling out all plans except descent. Ice on the tent guys indicated the mountain was out of condition. Packing the wet gear we shouldered the sacks and roped for the slippery descent. By good fortune we were able to see traces of our steps cut on the way up, so much axe work was saved. A thousand feet below we met the coolies on their way up. Goria and Sangia took most of the four loads between them, and it was amazing to see how easily they carried them.

Down in the grassy alp of camp the sun shone, making the place seem an earthly paradise. We spread our wet gear on the flowers and luxuriated, enjoying the sounds of singing birds as we tucked into a good meal of soup, chapatties, tea, and biscuits. Two rare birds frequented this camp, white-browed rose finches and a species known as glandara, a thrush-like bird of cobalt blue and black. We were sorry to leave for descent to the Base Camp.

Spring, it appeared, had come to our old home. Perched on a crag was a shahin falcon, dark like a peregrine, with a white collar. Lammergeier and griffon vultures soared around, and a camp follower in the shape of a jungle crow squawked near us. Nesting by the waterfall was a white-capped redstart. Flocks of sheep and goats had arrived from Malari to pasture on the growth of new grass.

A fine day following a misty wet night put us in mood for going up to South Lampak peak again. We knew the route and it seemed a pity not to follow it up if there was a chance of getting the summit. If the coolies had any objections, they did not show them. Cheerfully we left next morning.

We got the tent up just in time, as a cold rain and torrential hail swept over the grassy alp from the east, the first time wind had blown from that direction. Afternoon gave us a view of our rock buttress, steaming with vapour against a subsidiary cloud layer. Tirsuli had us gasping, as a fragment of ice ridge was revealed through a hole in porridge-like steam, higher in the sky than anyone could imagine. These spectacular effects kept us out till dusk.

We climbed next morning in sunshine, Goria leading all the way, closely followed by Pakir. Madbir had a bad leg but gamely climbed to the start of the rocks. Nurbir, although sick, carried on to the end. From our platforms on the snow cornice we looked to the amethyst of the Tibetan plateau. Jagged ridges swept upwards on both sides of us and we knew we were on the easiest route to the summit. The rock buttress which was the immediate problem of tomorrow looked incapable of stopping us.

But 3.30 a.m. brought a repetition of the conditions that had driven us off the mountain on our first attempt. This time we were determined to make a start on the rocks above, and at 5.30 a.m. we roped up for the snow *arête* leading to the crag.

To our disgust the rock was as flaky as pastry, much worse than on Uja Tirche. The stuff came away in handfuls. We snooped elsewhere, then McKinnon started up a couloir. The high angle and the possibility of falling stones forced him down. Wherever we tried was hopeless. Further, it was snowing and dense clouds were settling in. Even if we got up the crag, its descent, if covered in new snow, would be suicidal, for we would not be able to select the firmest holds. There was nothing for it but go down.

South Lampak peak had been a trial, but we had forced it to the limit of justifiable mountaineering. Using death-or-glory tactics we might have stood on its 20,750-foot summit. We retreated with no regrets, knowing we had done our best.

Now we were ready for what promised to be the most interesting part of the expedition, the traverse of the

Girthi Gorges.   As a change from high-altitude mountaineering its prospect cheered our spirits.   Travel is the
true delight of the Himalaya.   Now we were going to get
travel, plus the discovery of unknown country.

Perimal and Sangia were despatched to Malari to ensure
the return of goats and coolies.   We rested, taking stock
of food, writing, looking at birds, or listening to the rain ;
fully relaxed in the knowledge that we had done all we
could hope to do here.

CHAPTER IX

Into the Girthi

LIKE a procession of Orangemen headed by their goats, the Malari men came on the 12th July. There was excitement round the fire that night, high spirits, singing, and laughter. We joined in when we had had some of the stuff, for the " chang " bottle was circulating.

It was a different story in the morning. We had packed the loads and had cunningly inserted in each bundle about two pounds more than the agreed fifty pounds per man load, for we had more weight than coolies to carry it. Our trickery was discovered at once. These Malari wallahs carry a spring balance in their heads. The loads were slung down and the contents ejected. Only when the weight was exact would they budge.

The monsoon clouds that had afflicted us for days were dispersing as we argued. Down the glen, banks of cumulus lay on the slopes, adding richness to the greens and height to the snow peaks above them. At last the loads were picked up and we were off, to climb steeply through alps sprung to new life in the rains.

Acres of rock geraniums made a haze of blue on the hillsides, and clustering anywhere they could cluster, were reds, yellows, and whites of potentilla and saxifrages, forget-me-nots, meconopsis, and pincushion mosses studded with flowers of eye-like beauty. The damp ground brought out their scents.

This morning the Himalaya of imagination had come to

life. A dark blue, almost black, sky, and thrown against it, the peaks that had been our companions for the last three weeks, wrinkled, corniced, fluted ; their snow edges the embodiment of inaccessibility. Blocking the head of the glacier the 8000-foot curtain of Tirsuli hung in glistening folds, unclimbable, a curtain of ice suspended from a knife-blade summit ridge high above everything.

We sat on the shoulder of Uja Tirche and took our last look at that peak. Like the teeth of a monster its pin-nacles jutted against the sky. It seemed incredible that we had followed a route over them and up its twin sickles of ice to the pointed top.

A narrow track dropped in scree into the Girthi. A bulge blocked the view. Eagerly we set off to look round this bulge. It was like looking into another world, a vegetationless world, a world of naked rock that rose sheer on the north side 7000 feet from the river. On our side, the wall of Uja Tirche sent down a great buttress to make the most impressive ravine we had seen in India, a Grand Canyon of Colorado on a more vertical scale.

Yet for all the arid prospect, there were flowers at our feet as we rounded the next bluff, flowers that found foot-hold in stones. There was even a thistle like the true Scots variety. And roses that grew in a bower over our heads, with colours all the more rich in this steely country.

Suddenly we were faced with a drop, steep scree at first, becoming rock, slabby and at a steep angle. One could only call it rock climbing, for hands as well as feet had to be used, and the position was exposed.

Traversing along narrow shelves we came to a gully. Beyond its waterfall was a cave, the perfect place to spend the night. Quickly a tent platform was built up for us on the steep ground while the coolies staked a claim in the cave. As we ate our hoosh of lentils and onions, rice and wild rhubarb, we looked back at the way we had come. It was hard to believe there was a simple way through these tilted rock slabs.

It seemed as if every night was to be a party with the Malari men. Round a camp fire in the cave the " chang " bottle was once more circulating. This time we were presented with a bottle to ourselves. Poured into a Primus this native spirit would considerably improve the normal output of British Thermal Units of heat. Inside us it promoted a knowledge of Indian songs and quickened the memory of ribald ditties thought forgotten.

The sleepless night that followed was punctuated by many visits outside to see the stars give way to clouds and then to rain. But at 6 a.m. blue sky was breaking through. We were going to get another monsoon gift from the Gods.

The going was delightful—among a rock garden of stunted pines and sweet-scented shrubs. Above us, on both sides, the mist still played hide and seek. Great pinnacles loomed out of the cloud, gigantic, yet only fractional parts of the mountain wall above.

We were heading for a bluff with a cut in its crest which fell straight to the river, spectacular from a distance, astonishing at close quarters. Watching the coolies and the tiny specks of goats climb over the rocks from a snow-filled ravine, one appreciated the savagery of the country, especially when the view opened out to show a series of similar bluffs. The snow gullies worried the coolies, for the result of a slip was to slither to the lip of the snow and down over smooth walls. With good steps cut for them they were happy.

We rounded various tree-hung bluffs, with many ups and downs, and were amongst softer scenery of lesser gorges with a predominance of pines. These lesser gorges were deceptive, for the going became harder, more exposed to big drops, with long climbs to avoid landslides and descents to avoid crags. Luckily the sun continued to shine, revealing colours to great effect, for this would be a dreary place in bad weather. We dropped down to the river, near a place where a landslide had thrown a bridge across it, and climbed six hundred feet to cross a stream by a log bridge. Obviously the route was known to hill-men if not to Europeans.

We camped that night by the glacier torrent, not a bonny spot, nor a bonny river. Its water was the muddiest we had used to date. Tea made from it looked like soup. But as glacier water had so far done us no harm we drank it cheerfully.

The mystery of the bridge was solved. Near us was another bridge poised on two great rocks that jutted over the surging river. We crossed it, climbed twenty-five feet of steep earth poised dangerously above the water, and found ourselves on a crazy *arête* of conglomerate two hundred yards long leading to a bleak hillside showing signs of cultivation.

The settlement comprised two primitive thatched houses. Outside the houses were a couple of attractive women and a little girl. One of the young women had a baby at her breast. Thirteen pounds of potatoes was an unexpected bounty here, the potatoes coming out of a stone pit deep in the ground. The menfolk were away, but torn-up stones and juniper showed they were trying to add to the half square mile or so already reclaimed. Irrigation channels had been cunningly laid out. Altogether, a resourceful piece of colonization. The smiling women had a bad effect on our Dhotials who found it hard to keep away from the place.

We began next day with a rock scramble round various bluffs, till we reached another settlement, the place marked on the map as " Girthi ". It had long since been deserted, but was graced by a little temple in the form of a stone box. Little bells hung from its front, and suspended above it on a long stick was a larger bell. The coolies " salaamed " it, throwing inside odd coins, tobacco, and other treasures, to add to the collection of old knife-blades, cartridge cases, bits of tin, a mirror, and some magnificent fossils of ammonites and shells. These were sacrifices delivered up by past travellers to propitiate the Hindu gods.

As in every place where man has made his habitation, this place was distinguished by many birds, rosefinches, goldfinches, redstarts, wagtails, and warblers predominating.   Here we had to ford the river coming down from the Girthi glacier.   Not an easy passage.   I was given a lift across—on the back of the head coolie—and it was an exciting five minutes as he fought for footing, swaying and lurching with the water up to his middle.

An inexperienced traveller finds these rivers difficult. He tries to balance across, sliding his foot from one stone to the next.   In the Himalaya that spells disaster.   The boulders are moving with the rush of water, so the correct technique is to charge through.   To hesitate too long is to be swept away.

This green place was reminiscent of the Alps, with its narrow valley cutting into a hanging glacier showing through cloud.   There was a touch of Scotland too in the trailing mists and rain showers on the flower-covered slope above, which led us to a long upward traverse by stunted birch, and past a great landslide of rubble, to drop gradually to a pleasant alp knee-high in blue geraniums.

We headed off next morning for a grassy moraine which blocked the head of the gorge.   As we approached its top we heard a shout of joy from the men.   Ahead lay the promised land, a land quite different from that we had come through, a gentle glen, green like a Scottish strath, with the river splayed out in shingle beds.   The gorges were behind us.   On the meadows we could see two tents and herds of sheep.   The excitement of the coolies was more than for deliverance from the gorges.   They were hoping for the reward of a sheep.   We promised nothing, but waited to hear the price.

Down in the encampment we had a chat with three wild-looking shepherds.   For two fine sheep they wanted forty-six rupees (£3 9 0).   Our slender resources would not run to that extravagance, and one sheep was insufficient for our number.   We implied in our haggling that the

Himalayan hillman appears to have too deep a veneration for any animal a Sahib wants to buy, but the price remained unchanged. It was a disappointed convoy that crossed the river with wet shanks to camp that afternoon in a bleak corrie at 15,000 feet.

It was more than we deserved when, later in the day, Perimal, our head Dhotial, offered us a leg of mutton for the modest price of a few shillings. He had stayed behind to do a deal, and faithful to his sahibs, had passed over the spoil of a good bit of bargaining.

The route was now nearing its crux, the crossing of the Unta Dhura Pass at 17,800 feet, and to our sorrow the weather had set in bad for it. We climbed next day into a cloudy world of screes and rock. It was cold, and the rain felt wintry. Route-finding was not easy, but we trusted the map and kept on climbing. We doubted whether the Malari men had ever been thus far before, for it was obvious they depended on us. Then we heard the sound of bells that made us stop and listen.

Suddenly the mist opened and we saw above us, indistinct on the crest of a ridge, the forms of yaks, sheep, goats, and to our ears came the shouts of drovers. We had joined the Unta Dhura on the trade route, at the junction where north-east lies Tibet, and south-east is India.

As the clouds opened we saw the corrie was literally swarming with animals heading for Tibet, a traffic that churned up the mountainside to grey mud.

Coming towards us were wild-looking men, Tibetans, blue- or scarlet-robed, wearing long cloth boots and tall hats. Some were clad in skins and carried swords, others carried ancient muskets. By comparison the Bhotias—half-Tibetans who inhabit the Indian side of the range in the Goriganga—were gentry, neatly clad in homespuns, with striped waistcoats, jackets, and trousers of semi-European cut. This assorted party was a caravan gathered for self-protection against bandits. They would move into

Tibet together and camp as a party, their safety from attack being in their number.

Our coolies had moved well on the 2800-foot ascent. They did even better on the descent, for the going was difficult, down steep scree to the Safed glacier and across heart-breaking boulder-fields that seemed to have no ending.

There was a place marked " Bamlas " on the map. Our faith was pinned to it, but there was nothing to be seen when we got there, but glacier streams pouring through screes, a few boulders, and a profusion of sheep-droppings. There was no firewood so we had to go on.

The place marked on the map as " Dung " promised something. It was a green oasis in a rock desert, but still there was no firewood. A few more miles, and at last, 5000 feet down from the top of the pass and thirteen and a half miles from our camp of morning, we dug platforms for the tents. Juniper grew high above us, wet juniper that was unwilling to burn. Quickly the coolies laid in a stock and with mighty breaths fanned it to flame. They were in good heart despite ten hours' hard going over really punishing country. My only sorrow was that we had not a bottle of whisky among us, for they deserved a treat.

In rain next morning we sauntered into Milam village in the Goriganga. It was a delight to see fields, yellow with millet and fresh green, and in the centre, a well-built village of grey stone laid out in squares as a housing scheme. The scent in the air was curiously reminiscent of summer in England.

We were eager to get there. In that village which boasts the highest post office in India we expected our first mail from home for over three months. And we were eager to meet another Briton, Len Moules of the World-Wide Evangelization Crusade.

Followed by an increasing flock of men and children we were ushered past courtyards where were horses, piled saddle-bags, lounging Tibetans, and Bhotia women at work weaving carpets or grinding flour, to the house of the " Doctor Sahib ".

It was a pleasure to meet this virile man, and get news from home.   It was a mixed blessing though.   We learned for the first time that United Nations Forces were at war in Korea, and every newspaper of the large bundle presented by Moules shouted tension and unrest.

On the crest of the pass. Fixing the girths of the saddle-bags before dropping into the Girthi. South Lampak peak rises on the left

Above
The Girthi, a world of naked rock rising sheer, 7000 feet from the river

Left
Sometimes hands as well as feet were needed as can be seen from the sort of country shown here

Right
The third ravine in the Girthi Gorges. The route from the right comes across the snow gully and climbs by a steep scree shoot

The bridge across the river
to the Girthi settlement

In the Himalaya the rush
of water is such that the
stream bed moves with restless force, making footing
difficult. Scott is being
assisted over by a Bhotia

With fur bonnet on his head, the wild shepherd stands back while the sahibs and coolies inspect a sheep offered for sale

Camp on the Tibet border near the Unta Dhura Pass

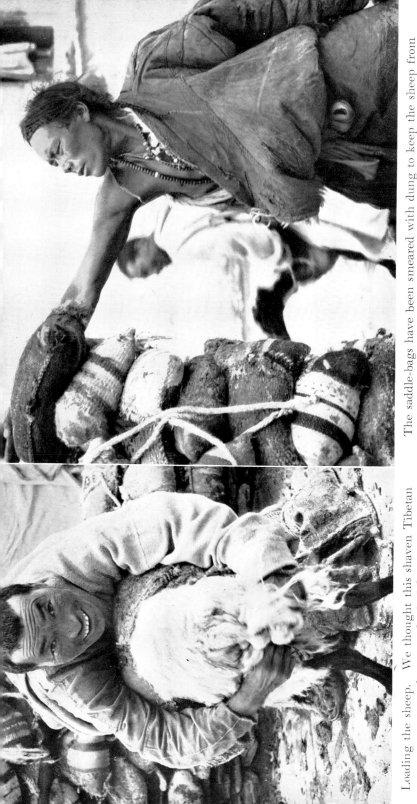

The saddle-bags have been smeared with dung to keep the sheep from nibbling

Below :

Clad in sheep-skins and long boots this wild-looking figure draws his sword with a smile. This is his protection against lama's ... ...

Loading the sheep. We thought this shaven Tibetan must be an unfrocked lama

Below :

Tibetan and Bhotia. The Bhotia is something of a dandy beside the cloaked figure of this Tibetan. Every Bhotia ...

Leonard Moules, missionary, in his little dispensary at Milam

A corner of Milam village

CHAPTER X

The Ralam Pass

THERE were many things we wanted to know from Moules. Had he ever been through the Girthi ? Had the monsoon officially broken ? How did the Bhotias live, and what was the nature of their society ? How was the trade with Tibet conducted ? Could we get coolies to go with us to the Darmaganga and what was the best route ? We were invited to lunch, when he would attempt to answer all our questions.

He had never been through the Girthi, nor had heard of any other European having been through. It looked as if ours was the first crossing and we thought it so until arrival back in Britain, when we discovered that it had, in fact, been crossed once before, in 1893 by Dr. Kurt Boeckh. Moules' date for the monsoon coincided with the bad weather that had pinned us down on South Lampak peak. On the Bhotias he was a mine of information.

This valley of the Goriganga used to be Tibet, he told us, the name given to it being the Johar Bhot, as was also the Darma Bhot where we were going. The Bhotias of Milam get all their living by trade, each family having three houses, one at Milam, one lower down at Mansairi, and one fifty miles down on the edge of the hills. Right now the male population were preparing a caravan to Tibet, with grain and manufactured goods, animals and spices, to trade for rugs, trinkets, salt, and borax.

In October, they would move down the valley to dispose

of their goods at a big fair held in November. Winter would drive them down to their lowest quarters till April, when the upward cycle would begin again.

We had no experience of the Milam Bhotias as yet, but judging them by the Malari wallahs they must be men of enterprise, able to travel hard, across gorges, over high passes, and to ford dangerous rivers. Moules, who loved them, praised their qualities but struck a sombre note. Venereal disease and alcohol were destroying the Bhotia race. Drunkenness and promiscuity were rife, he said, and it was impossible to make headway against them. Ninety per cent have gonorrhoea, and there is quite a lot of tuberculosis. Sometimes he handled over a hundred medical cases a day. Although not a fully qualified doctor he was able to perform cataract operations.

This was in many ways a sad day, it was our last with Tom McKinnon and the Malari wallahs. We had grown fond of the latter and were sorry to see them go. Tom was a more vital loss. He was not only a tower of strength to the party, but the cheeriest personality in it. Characteristically, he chose to go home by Trail's Pass over the shoulder of Nanda Kot, in preference to the valley route. He set off with one coolie and no tent. As rain and clouds swept the glen our hearts bled for him.

Not for a few days did we find out what had happened in the continuously bad weather that followed his departure. He had attempted the pass, but after two nights soaked to the skin, had been forced to give it up by his coolie refusing to go any further. A soiled note delivered to us by a strong-looking Bhotia told us he was trying the ordinary route by Mansairi.

Events were shaping nicely with us. Moules had " laid-on " coolies who were willing to attempt a crossing of the Ralam Pass, despite the fact that the Ralam had been crossed only a few times in history and only once * in the monsoon. They contracted to cross it with forty-pound

* See *Throne of the Gods* by Gannser and Heim.

loads in six days. The Ralam is really a succession of three passes, crossing the main Himalayan chain at 18,470 feet, providing a quick route from the Goriganga to the Darmaganga.

Ideally we should have made this move after the monsoon, the object of our crossing being to reach a group of unclimbed mountains known as the Panch Chuli. Our hopes were fastened on the highest peak, Panch Chuli, 22,650 feet, which we had hoped to attempt in September.

A balance of cash showed we would need to telescope our scheme. The date was mid-July, and the high cost of food and coolies provided no alternative but pushing our plans in the monsoon or going home. Bad weather or no, we would try the Ralam and the Panch Chuli.

First of all we wanted to say farewell to Moules, and see the " going-away " party arranged in his honour. It was rumoured there were to be dancing girls, sword dancers, and drummers. There was plenty to see in Milam while we waited, Tibetan sheep being clipped, the spinning of carpets, and the Mani wall with its carved lotus flowers and inscriptions in Tibetan where followers of Buddha could intone their prayers as they passed. The Chowkidar of Milam was an ancient Tibetan, much too old to make the seasonal journeys up and down the valley. During the winter when snow buried the houses to roof-top level he lived by himself in an upstairs room.

The sound of drums next morning sent us speeding to the village. Standing on roofs and crowding the narrow streets, the whole population had turned out. In the centre of it all were the musicians and two rather attractive singers. The band consisted of an instrument like a piano-accordion and a square violin played with a bow. They struck up as we arrived.

The dancing consisted of body-swaying and sensuous movements of the hands in time to the music. Through half-closed eyes the two girls managed to get the maximum of sexual excitement into their simple song and dance.

Their concession to the dance was in little shuffling steps delivered with a tap of the shoe. Now and again they would break into song, the five drummers on such occasions beating louder and louder.

Then the sword dancers took a hand. Again, dancing was a misnomer. The swords were merely brandished and whirled about, though one of the male dancers tip-toed on neat steps. The other swordsman made faces fierce and comic. Sometimes the music stopped, and the comedian would deliver a pantomime which sent the crowds in roars of laughter with his funny faces. The highlight was when he whirled his sword so effectively that it swung out of his hand to cleave the crowd. Beyond a couple of juvenile heads being cut open there was no real damage done.

The appearance of Moules with his laden jopas was the signal for the procession to move forward. A garland of flowers was hung round his neck, the girl dancers swaying round him and the musicians playing ever more furiously as they advanced slowly through the village to mount the col which was the beginning of his journey. Blank cartridges were fired and synchronized to perfection with the final of an exciting drum tattoo.

The exchange of many rupees, handshaking all round, and Moules was off, lighter in pocket, on his way to Bampa by the long northward route over the bleak passes of the Tibet border to the Dauli Valley. An offer to serenade us back to camp was refused as being too expensive in bakhshish.

We had enjoyed our stay at Milam. A sheep had been killed and eaten, the Dhotials were sufficiently rested, and everyone was keen to be on the move again. Came the morning of 25th July and the Milam wallahs arrived to carry our kit.

The first ten miles were pleasant, on a path, turfy and fairly flat, curling into village fields of yellow flowering millet where Himalayan greenfinches and goldfinches sported, the latter not quite so beautiful as the British bird.

Red-billed choughs replaced the Alpine choughs of Milam, rufus turtle doves inhabited the trees, and wagtails flitted by the numerous streams. We might have been in the Scottish Highlands.

We camped that night in a little glen at 10,400 feet, between high ridges, the southerly one 5000 feet above us being our first pass of tomorrow. This day was celebrated in unusual style with mushrooms and fried eggs, then a great pot of potatoes plus the remaining leg of the sheep we had slaughtered, finishing up with a vast dumpling made to a recipe that had reached me in Milam.

There were wonderful effects next morning as the sunlight chased the mist from glistening wet crags. Our spirits were high as we climbed through flowers and shrubs for 3000 feet, then up a bare corrie for another 2000 feet to reach the crest of the ridge in rain. Down steeply, to contour a couple of snow gullies and trace a way through knee-deep flowers past a huge waterfall, and we were among the perched houses of Ralam village 3000 feet below the pass.

Mud and dung were our chief impressions as we walked through, for no attempt had been made to provide paving in this outlandish settlement of thatched houses. Most of the men were away in Tibet trading, but the few who greeted us were very friendly, the women peeking out of doors and round corners to look at these bearded visitors from another world.

The camp just outside the village was dispensary and object of wonder to everyone. Sore heads, sore tummies, sore eyes, are complaints imagined or endured by every inhabitant of the Himalaya. Luckily the expedition's Health Service was able to dispense medicine to the needy, but malingerers were quickly identified and sent packing with a halibut oil capsule.

Our visit was so much an occasion here that when it was time to leave at 7 a.m. a procession was formed in our honour. Heading it were the boys of the village, who approached hands clasped in an attitude of prayer, chanting a little song to the rhythm of four drummers. We took our places behind, and in a long column wound round the hillside to a drum rhythm which grew more and more exciting. Stimulated by it the drummers gyrated now and then, kicking their heels as in the polka.

Then the kiddies plucked handfuls of flowers to use in a dance, a bouquet in each hand being flourished to emphasize arm movements as they interwound round each other in what I took to be a traditional figure.

We came to a flat place where a ring was formed and the drums dinned more furiously. Here each kiddy was pushed into the ring to perform a solo. One imitated a monkey hunting for fleas, another made funny faces, while others flung themselves about, whirling fiercely in true Highland fling style.

One little toddler I noticed had intruded himself several times into the dance on the way along the path, so I pushed him in for a solo. He gave a most inspiring performance, getting the arm movements correctly and twisting and turning till he overbalanced amidst loud cries of approval.

The ceremony was over now, farewells were exchanged, and rather touched by this spontaneous tribute we made our way to the snout of the Shunkalpa glacier. Flowers are my chief memory of this place. Right to the snout of the glacier they were knee-deep, continuing in small Alpines among the stones to an even thicker array up the steep hillside, where we saw our first Himalayan blue poppies, delicate things of delphinium blue.

Over a col, we came to a magic little alp gay with primulas. Our arrival was well timed, for heavy cloud and rain set in the moment the tent was down.

We were a straggling column next morning, our own coolies, Ralam coolies who carried wood for cooking, and the Bhotias from Milam, to the number of twenty-one, trailing over half a mile of misty hillside. It was a hard climb on loose scree enlivened by a sudden clearing, revealing the cleft of our pass on the rock ridge. Northwards as we climbed, the peaks of the Tibet border cleared, showing their glaciers to great effect.

But the real thrill was looking down to the Yanckchar glacier, the highway which would take us over the ridge to the Darma. It was an exciting route, ringed round by ice peaks whose icefalls hung down steeply from enclosing crags. A long halt up here waiting for the porters and we slid down swiftly on scree to the hard going of the glacier.

We camped on flat stones near a couple of snow beds. A fox, fawn-coloured with an enormous brush of lighter colour, was a surprise in this Arctic wilderness. A more unpleasant surprise was a sudden shift of wind to the south, bringing sleet, hail, thunder, and lightning, and lowering the temperature immediately. Owing to the wet, the coolies could not make their chapatties, and we felt mis-givings about the morrow with 3000 feet of glacier and icefall to climb, and 5000 feet of reputedly difficult ground to descend on the other side of the pass. Hail still battered down as we retired.

Moonlight flooding the tent awakened me. In the in-credible silence the peaks stood clear of cloud, silvery above vast shadows. Frost rang below my boots as I walked round the camp. To put the mood of these mighty peaks —all of them unclimbed—into words is impossible, especially now that all doubts for the morning had been cleared up.

Firewood trouble prevented an early start, the coolies sitting wrapped up in blankets while smoke poured from lifeless fires. For us it gave opportunities of photographs as the pale glaciers and ice flutings took on the burnish of dawn.

At 7.30 a.m. we started up the moraine to reach an icefall cut by a huge crevasse. Warmed up, the men were in great form, competing with each other in the cutting of steps upward and across this slippery obstacle. We merely followed, marvelling how sure-footed these men were in such an assortment of footgear, sandals made from rubber tyres, plimsols, unnailed leather shoes, etc.

Round a bend in the glacier, more sliding on moraine, and ahead of us and only 1200 feet above, was the summit of the pass, very steep and rocky at the top, and cut by prominent snow gullies. The glacier approach looked good, but we were worried for our men's eyes, for we could issue only a few pairs of snow goggles. They surprised us by producing raw wool, teased it out to make a band, and pulled the wool over their eyes.

This last lap was hard going, the sliding stones and high angle telling at this altitude. Heat was fierce too. Yet I would put it on record that one of our permanent Dhotials, on arriving on the col, went back immediately to help another man who was making heavy weather of the ascent.

Impressions on the other side of the pass were of massed rain clouds, thousands of feet deep, above which we caught glimpses of pointed rock peaks and snowy heads. Descent was amusing. Steep scree led to glacier ice thinly covered in snow, and Goria, our best coolie, lost no time in sledging down his load. The others followed, whooping with joy in the rush of speed, themselves and the baggage taking a few tumbles in the process.

Falling stones rattling down from the steep crags on the west called for vigilance since this was our route. We moved fast, down a slippery ice course, to traverse over the glacier and glissade to narrowing rock walls where in these misty confines the mountain had its last fling. Boulders hurtled towards our last three coolies. They ran hard and escaped with nothing more than a fright.

There was no direct descent from here, a traverse over the westerly rock shoulder taking us on to an airy perch on the vast rock wall leading to the 20,840-foot peak above. A sudden clearing showed our route down 1000 feet of steepish rocks to the Nipchukang glacier, where only a mile or so away we could see green grass bordering its boulder-strewn course.

om McKinnon who left us at
Iilam to try the crossing of Trail's
Pass

he coolies used their rest days in
Iilam to good purpose by making
iemselves new trousers and add-
ıg length to an outsize bedmat

Sangia is proud of this pullover he has finished.
Another is already on the needles

Perimal spinning on the march. The twirling
spindle takes up the spun wool from the raw fleece
on his wrist

The dancing girls of Milam sway to the rhythm of weird music

On the Ralam Pass. The route crossed over the rock curtain in the middle distance

A telephoto shot of the Yankchar Pass showing the peaks Chhiring We and Suli Top (left and right) behind

On the crest of the Ralam Pass at 18,470 feet showing the downward route

The Panch Chuli range from the base camp. Our attempt was on the highest right-hand peak, 22,650 feet

Camp 2 on Panch Chuli

Near Camp 2 on Panch Chuli we came across this settlement, a couple of primitive huts on the edge of the glacier. The gift of a biscuit tin causes great excitement

Camp 4 on Panch Chuli. Monsoon clouds welling up over the Tibetan peaks

The glacier at 19,000 feet and the ice walls of Panch Chuli. The main peak, 22,650 feet, rises on the right. Its summit ridge was a transparent icicle

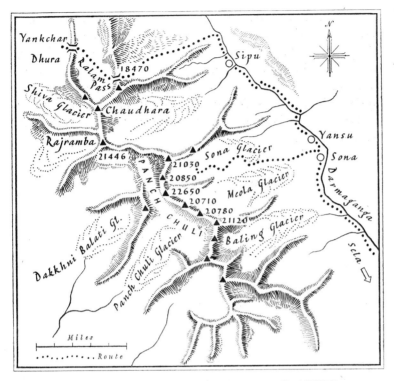

FROM THE RALAM PASS TO PANCH CHULI

There was elation in the party as we descended to where juniper wood grew out of the steep hillside above us. The time was only 4.45 p.m. so the crossing had occupied only nine hours. Miraculously, only one coolie complained of eye trouble.

It was cloudy when we left next morning for the steep descent to the Lassar Yankti glen. It was rather a tortuous route with a deep scree ravine to cross, gradually becoming more verdant till we were among rose bushes and stunted birch where rosefinch flocks foraged and Himalayan ruby-throats sang exuberantly. The valley floor seemed impossibly far down, the effect being emphasized by writhing monsoon clouds which streamed down from 20,000-foot ridges, leaving 10,000-foot gaps to the river.

G

At length we were beside it, and in a couple of miles saw ahead of us a cluster of houses above neat terraces of pink and yellow flowering millet.   Steep woods clinging to the hillside gave an extraordinary verdant atmosphere to this village of Sipu.   Our camp was placed by a mountain spring where we could most appreciate its infinite beauty.

We had arrived at the first reconnaissance point for Panch Chuli.

CHAPTER XI

Panch Chuli

A MAJOR Himalayan peak is so large, and the scale and angle of its slopes so misleading, that any reconnaissance of it means climbing an adjacent peak.   We could not see Panch Chuli from our Sipu camp.   It was screened from us by a rock peak 19,610 feet, a veritable castle of rock towers situated on a fortress of red rock.   If we could climb this peak and were granted a view, we would know a few of the answers to an ascent of Panch Chuli.   The first job was to make a reconnaissance of it.

Murray had to stay in camp to sort out a pay wrangle with the Milam men.   Scott and I could hardly wait to get off.   The peaks were orange flushed against a pale sky, and the millet fields were shining pink and yellow against a back-cloth of sun-brilliant birches topped by a 21,000-foot ice peak.   The time was only 7 a.m.

We climbed swiftly, but not swiftly enough.   At 15,000 feet the monsoon clouds had won the race, the blackness of thunder filling the glen.   In such ominous conditions we turned for home, the deluge beginning as we reached the lower glacier drenching us as we made our best speed on the difficult ground of boulders and steep scree.   It was invigorating to feel the fresh rain on one's cheek and forget the wet skin beneath one's clothes.

The rain continued most of next day, but it was not a dreary day for Murray.   As medicine man, his services were required in Sipu village, and he filled his rucksack

G*

with our few remaining stores.   Most of the Sipu women
were old hags, the most interesting part of them being the
ornaments which clung to ears, ankles, necks, breasts, etc.;
we did not brave the rain to follow.

We missed a treat.   His first cases were sore bellies,
nothing intangible either, the marks were plain to see,
round sores like old vaccination marks.   He searched the
medicine bag and found Castellani's Paint, the cure for
foot rot, a bright colour pleasing to the eye and pleasing
to the ornamental taste of the Sipu ladies.   The bottle was
nearly empty of its purple contents by the time he had
slapped it on rank and file, for no one wanted to miss his
deft brush.

His next case was dental, the mere withdrawing of a
tooth.   Our forceps for upper and lower jaw had been used
for withdrawing nails out of packing cases until this date.
He found the tooth a more difficult substitute despite
a willing patient.   So far as we know the old dame
still carries the tooth, and the story of its unsuccessful
withdrawal circulates wherever " chang " bottles are
opened.

Nothing could be gained by staying up here in the
rain, except a bad reputation, so we moved down to the
foot of our mountain, on the assumption that if a spell
of good weather came, we would try it, with or without
reconnaissance.

The first glimpse was inspiring.   Below us were the
rooftops of a village, with a glacier stream running through
lush meadows to the abrupt snout of the lowest glacier we
had seen in the Himalaya.   Above that, looming into cloud,
a tangle of icefalls discharging water in thousand-foot leaps
over crags.   Somewhere up there was the 22,650-foot peak
we hoped to climb.   This Alpine glen was the perfect place
for a base camp.

Morning brought us a breath-taking sight of the whole
range.   Rising over 12,000 feet from our camp in rock
faces, crevassed ridges, fierce bulges, we saw them as superb

but uncompromising peaks, from the twin ice spears in the south-east to the soaring point north-west we hoped to reach. Murray took advantage of the clearing by making a quick reconnaissance sketch while Scott and I climbed 2000 feet to reconnoitre the approach. There would be no difficulty about Camp 2, we found.

Camp 2 was pitched next day on a grassy shelf above the glacier, a place where we were surprised to find three primitive huts in occupation by a cheery family. Presumably they look after the sheep and cows which graze this upland situated so dramatically between thundering waterfalls and overlooking a glacier.

The climb up to Camp 3 was absorbing, first by a steep grass rake between cliffs, then through knee-deep flowers to rocks where the coolies could show off their rock climbing skill. It was good to get level with high-looking rock peaks and see at close hand the tremendous glaciation of this cirque of mountains. Camp was pitched in mist on a snow bed, but we managed 1500 feet of recce of the next day's route before retiring. Despite thunder and lightning and heavy rain in the night we were very snug at 16,000 feet.

Dawn came with dense mist and occasional glimpses of shadowy mountain walls around us. Climbing steeply we climbed to a spot where we thought the icefall should be breached. Our two coolies did not like the look of its crevassed face, but there was no alternative and we soon talked them into doing it. With good steps and the rope for safeguard, there was no real danger. It was the mist and feeling of great height that made them reluctant.

Luckily there was a clearing which enabled us to see the route beyond to the great icefall of the Sona glacier. A convenient shelf between steep ice above and a slope seamed with crevasses below, led us to a tangled mass of *séracs*, rather a ferocious-looking place.

Again the coolies were wavering, but a little flattery, plus the more tangible rewards of bars of chocolate, jollied

them sufficiently for them to pick up their bags once more.
With sixty-pound loads they needed such support.

Where to tackle the icefall was the problem.   We went
left, up a little snow *arête*, then downward and to the
right to avoid an artillery of hanging stuff poised above.
This was a good route, only complicated by enveloping
cloud.

Goria announced he was finished, waving his hand to
indicate he could go no further, but stimulated by thirty-
six year old Sangia's example he staggered on to the end
of his tether, where a mass of crevasses would have prevented us taking them further anyhow.   Giving them a
rope and a warning to stick to the steps of the morning
we said our farewells and shouldered the kit.

But the conditions were too uncertain to push very much
further up an unknown glacier so full of potential dangers
as this one.   As it was, our camp was pitched between two
crevasses at approximately 19,000 feet.

Then came a most marvellous clearing, disheartening
from a climbing standpoint.   Panch Chuli threw off its
cloud and the sun came out to show us the wonders of this
upper basin.   At its glacier head, close to us, was our col
which we had hoped would be a walk.   It rose sheer for
nearly a thousand feet, the ice at the foot of the rock bear-
ing the grooves of continual avalanche.   Also, the ridge
rising from it to the summit gleamed transparent in the
sunshine—ice—two thousand feet of it, at an angle where
every step would need to be cut by ice-axe.   This was not
the route to the top of Panch Chuli.

Nevertheless the effects on this ice mountain were worth
coming for.   Below us, the clouds were seething in masses
of cumulus, great towers of it which wound round the red-
grey Tibetan ridges and snow peaks above.   One caught
glimpses of grass hillsides so impossibly far down and so
brilliantly coloured, out of this world of rock and ice, it
was hard to believe we were part of the same earth.   We
retired to the tent for shelter from the fierce sun, yet three

The skirts of Panch Chuli. The " pleats " are caused by avalanches

Camp at 19,000 feet on Panch Chuli. Scott takes a reading with his meter to try to gauge the brilliance of the light at these heights

The north col, Panch Chuli. This curtain of stone-swept rock nearly 1000 feet high turned the party back

Murray and Scott are fêted by the Bhotias of Yansu. After cups of hot milk and native spirit the drums were brought out and played enthusiastically for hours on end

This is the favourite instrument of the Bhotias. Unfortunately this one had only two working notes which gave it a certain monotony

The last of Panch Chuli

hours later my feet were cold in three pairs of socks. All night long avalanches fell.

Next day we climbed through crevasses towards the col to assure ourselves we were not being merely " chicken-hearted ". Stones falling continually showed our judgement had been sound. Freak conditions of snow showers and enervating heat alternated till sunset, when gold clouds spread their warmth over the avalanche flutings hanging above the tent.

The night which followed was far from comfortable. Snow pattered on the tent continually, and the intermittent crash and rumble of avalanches prevented sleep. It was by no means a dull wait for dawn, much more like being in the thick of an air-raid.

In an Arctic landscape of poor visibility we packed up the tent and led downwards, probing for hidden crevasses and cutting steps where necessary. With heavy loads, the climb to the icefall seemed considerable, and the rock and scree slope below uncommonly steep. The faithful Sangia and Goria met us a few hundred feet from camp, grinning from ear to ear at our safe return.

Halting for tea, we pushed down to Camp 1, a total descent of 7000 feet. For the first time in two days we felt a desire to eat. The green meadows, the camp fire, and the luxury of a large tent were appreciated as never before. I had had my fill of Panch Chuli. So had Murray.

Scott, the born explorer, had other ideas. Nothing would satisfy him but a visit to the glacier coming down from the south col. This meant a climb upward of 4000 feet but, nothing daunted, he proposed it for the morrow. Such enthusiasm could not be let down, and Murray proposed going up with him while I went down and re-established the Base Camp.

They made their reconnaissance in thick weather, but saw enough to satisfy themselves that this was the route to the south col. The climbing looked difficult, but they think Panch Chuli will be climbed by this route. They did not think it was a route for Dhotials, unaccustomed as they are to difficult ice climbing and high-altitude mountaineering.

For us, the climbing part of the expedition was over.

CHAPTER XII

The Road Back

THE sting of defeat on Panch Chuli was mitigated by the rain and clouds which formed a black wall at the head of the valley. Across the glen spasms of sunshine lit the millet fields, gleaming in chess-board pattern under great wreaths of coiling vapours that hung white on the dark mountain walls. One never feels so bad at leaving a place if the weather is bad, but we had grown to love this glen.

With the engagement of two local coolies our preparations for the hundred-and-fifty-mile trek back to civilization were completed, but first of all we were invited to the village for a celebration timed to begin at 8 a.m. The word " dud " (milk) had been mentioned, so we felt we were in for a spree.

In pouring rain next morning we were ushered into a house to sit on a carpeted dais. Very soon we were in a daze, as a wall of brown faces was pushed nearer and nearer to us, the pressure from the rear continuing as more and more newcomers squeezed in to get a look at us. Not knowing a word of the language we could do no more than smile and murmur " Thik ", or vary it by nodding a knowing head.

It was a relief when native cigarettes were handed round. None of us are smokers, and you want to be a smoker to smoke these narrow gaspers. Into the bargain you require a strong pair of lungs to promote combustion, for they are wrapped in a dark plant leaf stiff as brown

95

paper. We puffed and coughed and were glad when a basin of dirty grey liquid was produced. Three little silver cups were filled and handed to us. Saying " Cheers " to the multitude we drank.

Drinking the stuff was easy compared to the effort of holding it down. It was a relief to get to the bottom of the cup and look pleasant about it. To my horror the cup was promptly seized and refilled. Then the " chang " made its appearance. It tasted like vinegar and burnt with inspiring fire.

Under its influence I was invited to play an instrument like a piano-accordion with a little bellows attached. My attempted rendering of " I can wash a sailor's shirt " was foiled by broken keys. Only two notes appeared to be working. Operating these two, one of the Bhotias intoned a monotonous chant. All that was missing was the snake.

Then we heard the sound of drums—no " chang " mirage either—for the drummers were lined up outside to accompany us down to the village square. Squatting on a large mat, ourselves seated on carpets, the drummers began a long tattoo. It was so long I decided it was time to give them something in return. The crowd stood round expectantly while I collected the drums in a semi-circle round me.

Wielding a couple of great sticks I beat out rhythms fast and furious, but my art appeared to be lost on them for there were no cries of encore. They looked baffled rather than amused. A " Joe Daniels " was evidently not appreciated here. Anyhow, as one who used to take his drumming very seriously, I enjoyed whacking the skins, and had there been a spare drum would have joined the band that marched us back to camp.

Next day we were off, to stroll down a fine path and enter a different kind of scenery, a scenery of wooded bluffs and ravines falling to millet fields on the shelves above an earth-pinnacled canyon. The ice of the Baling glacier, projecting far below the tree line in the lowest glacier we had seen in India, was the only hint of snow peaks. Mountains of cloud buried Panch Chuli.

The wooded glen cut deeper and deeper, becoming a ravine on a tremendous scale. Rock pinnacles jutted above thousands of feet of trees, and great crags disappeared into cloud. The path wound past gleaming slabs and lush flowering shrubs. After the bleakness of the two other Tibetan trade routes we had seen, this one was a revelation.

All the time we were losing height, the tropical vegetation, red and grey monkeys, banana palms, and sunbirds testifying to this if the hothouse atmosphere was not testimony enough. It was exciting one day to round a corner and look on a green wall scored by rock gullies, and beyond, seas of forest that disappeared in the grey of monsoon clouds—Nepal.

It was a wild path, crossing under waterfalls, climbing like a staircase in places, at other times spanning drops on wooden planks, a narrow gangway contouring a complexity of rivers and foothills. Five days from the Base Camp and we were able to buy mangos, ripe bananas, and delicious Indian corn for roasting, while we waited for torrential rain to subside and let us resume our journey.

We were lucky to beat this rain by one day, for the track we had descended was now impassable by landslides and rushing torrents. We had found these streams just fordable the wet day before, the result of a slip in the thigh-deep water being to go over falls and land, perhaps, in the roaring river below. Certainly I have never known such fast-flowing water.

The walk to Almora now took us over a succession of jungle ridges, none of them above 6500 feet, and most of them considerably lower. Butterflies swarmed on the paths, large swallow-tailed varieties big as warblers, some with black forks and blue wings, some black with red tails, yellow ones with blue vents, and smaller varieties that went about in whirlwinds, little sprites, dancing madly, to settle on dung like flowers newly opened. The humid air was strong with honey scents.

Birds were everywhere, kingfishers, bulbuls, red-billed magpies, shrikes, flycatchers, spotted forktails, black-headed sibia, crested hawk eagle, pigmy owlet, drongos, pigeons, etc. It was a naturalist's paradise. Once I interrupted a bear hunt, but to the disgust of the hunters I had no gun. With clubs, spears, and dogs, they beat the undergrowth, and were still at it when I left them.

Holy men *en route* from Tibet to India were colourful figures on this path. We had many interesting talks as we drank tea together at the wayside howffs which distinguish this busy low route.

To these men, the body is nothing, the present is nothing, war is nothing, if the ultimate truth that each man has a greater self is realized. Ambition, lust, greed, comfort, ego, these are only a few of the things that stand between man and his creator.

The " inner joy " is their goal, oneness with God, not necessarily a Hindu god but a Universal God. They have no doubt about reincarnation. One life is too short to attain the ultimate, according to them.

One evening after heavy rain Panch Chuli came out of the clouds. It was the first time we had seen it since leaving Sona, a point of snow utterly removed from the earth, dwarfing the foothills and towering over the blurred shapes of immense foothills. A fortnight ago we had been camped under its crest, enduring heat and glare, which added to the effects of altitude and loss of appetite had been wellnigh insufferable.

The natives call these effects " the poison of the heights ". We had tasted this poison, and been glad to get away, to live again at lower levels and exult in the wonderful feeling of physical energy in daily marches through a beautiful country. Yet, one view was sufficient to flood the mind with longing to go back, the discomforts forgotten, the revelation of the heights beckoning.